How to Cure
a Hangover

'Three bowls do I mix for the temperate: one to health, which they empty first, the second to love and pleasure, the third to sleep. When this bowl is drunk up, wise guests go home. The fourth bowl is ours no longer, but belongs to violence; the fifth to uproar, the sixth to drunken revel, the seventh to black eyes, the eighth is the policeman's, the ninth belongs to biliousness, and the tenth to madness and the hurling of furniture.'

EUBULUS, 375BC

bread before downing several pints or drinking a bottle of wine is about as much use as trying to put out a heath fire with a bucket of water. It's the butter, ham or egg in the sandwich that will keep a drinker on his or her feet.

In countries such as France, Italy and Spain, where drinking with meals is much more common than bar-side drinking, potential ill-effects from alcohol are much less common. The explanation for this is more complex than the effect eating has on stomach-emptying time and the rate of absorption of the alcohol.

If a drinker is starving when he starts his evening's entertainment, his liver is less efficient at producing ADH. Alternatively, somebody who is already well-fed before setting out has a liver already geared up to launch the alcohol-metabolizing ADH enzymes, and the alcohol, — whenever it is absorbed — is metabolized more quickly and efficiently.

How to Cure
a Hangover

Andrew Irving

First published in the United Kingdom in 2004 by Little Books Ltd,
48 Catherine Place, London SW1E 6HL

10 9 8 7 6 5 4 3 2 1

A CIP catalogue record for this book is available from the British Library.

ISBN: 1 904435 45 9

The author and publisher will be grateful for any information that will assist them
in keeping future editions up-to-date. Although all reasonable care has been taken in the
preparation of this book, neither the publisher, editors nor the author can accept any liability
for any consequences arising from the use thereof, or the information contained therein.

Every attempt has been made to trace any copyright holders. The publishers extend their
gratitude to all those who have contributed to the recipe suggestions in this book.

Special thanks to Phil Moad of the Kobal Collection for picture research, and to
all those at the Kobal Collection for their generous support and cooperation.

Many thanks to:
Jamie Ambrose for editorial production and management,
Debbie Clement and Mousemat Design Limited for jacket and text design,
Claudia Dowell for proofreading.
Printed in China by SNP Leefung Printers Limited.

Contents

'I'd hate to be a teetotaller. Imagine getting up in the morning and knowing that's as good as you're going to feel all day.'

DEAN MARTIN

What is a Hangover?

Nine out of ten people enjoy a drink. Most of them only usually drink in moderation and they wake next morning feeling active, alert and even refreshed after an evening spent away from the usual routine. Yet even people with the most ordered lifestyle occasionally step out of line once in a while. They have more to drink than their bodies can cope with. Noxious chemicals accumulate and damage the system. Alcohol in excess is a poison, and its symptoms are known as the 'hangover'. It is all that is left over from the party.

Although the term 'hangover' is no more than a hundred years old, the symptoms to which it refers are as old as alcohol itself. Brewing and distilling are thought to have started in the Middle East, but whoever claims the credit for first discovering the joys of drinking, it is certain that alcohol has played its part in social life throughout the world for at least twelve thousand years.

For as long as there have been drinking parties, there have been hangovers. Mead was being drunk in Syria before 10,000 BC and beer was being brewed not long afterwards. In fact, beer was so highly prized in the Middle East that the term for it, *kash*, lives on today as 'cash'. Just as Roman soldiers were later paid with salt (from which the term 'salary' is derived), so beer was part of the cash with which the labourers who built the pyramids received their reward.

The day after payday, it's fairly certain that at least some of the labourers in the desert, the Roman soldiers in the Middle East or the hunter-gatherers in northern Europe would have been nursing a hangover. There is always a price to pay for drinking to excess, whether it has been part of a daily routine, or because there has been an occasion to celebrate. The amount someone can drink before they become intoxicated, and the depth of intoxication to which they can descend, varies from person to person. But if someone exceeds his or her limits, the symptoms suffered are the same now as they were ten thousand years ago.

Clubbers hitting the local town on a Friday or Saturday night will be suffering the following morning in the same way as executives who have been celebrating the end of another office week with a dinner party. Similarly, the old boozer who has spent a lonely evening with only a couple of bottles of claret to keep him company will not be looking forward to his bacon and eggs anymore than the twenty-year-old designer who caught a taxi home at 3AM after a night of constant vodka and cranberry.

How Alcohol Affects the Body

Alcohol in moderate quantities eases inhibitions, relaxes the drinker, increases the sense of well-being and in general makes for a good party. Like any medicine, if it is taken inappropriately or in unwise amounts, the effects are not so pleasant. Even in relatively modest amounts – just a drink or two – the inhibited but insecure or angry person may become aggressive.

Anyone who takes too much alcohol will find that, in excess, it acts as a poison to every system of the body. It makes the kidneys secrete more urine so that the body becomes generally dehydrated. It inflames the stomach and guts and causes a chemical gastro-enteritis, so the person feels sick, is sometimes sick and finds it difficult to move too far from the bathroom the next day.

Alcohol also has a marked effect on brain cells. While drinking, it already begins to affect brain cells. Fortunately, not enough is taken to kill them, but it does damage them and incapacitates them – hence the increasing lack of sense that the drinker makes as he rambles on with a slurred voice. Inhibitions are lessened – although admittedly some of us are so inhibited that we are dead drunk before they all disappear. The drinker's mood changes and varies as the level of drunkenness increases.

The effect on people's moods can be illustrative of their underlying personalities. A well-controlled and socially adept person may be the life and soul of the party before drinking, but if the same person is tense, yet normally hides aggression, a couple of drinks may unleash emotions that friends never knew existed. Such people become bad-tempered, antisocial, foul-mouthed and paranoid.

Likewise, the inability to walk without staggering, or even to focus the eyes, increases as consumption increases. The damage to the brain cells also causes a swelling of the brain as the cells themselves swell. Every other part of the body becomes dehydrated, but the brain becomes waterlogged – it no longer fits neatly into the skull. As it becomes compressed, the headache that is often the first sign of an impending hangover begins.

Alcohol also upsets the body's control of sugar. Our very existence is dependent on the checks and balances that people have to maintain a comparatively steady amount of glucose circulating in the bloodstream. In response to the intake of sugar-rich alcohol, the pancreas produces large quantities of insulin. Once the person has stopped drinking, the high levels of insulin are still circulating, so that the blood-sugar level is dramatically reduced. The body has overreacted to the glucose in the alcohol by producing too much insulin, and this causes a rebound effect on the blood-sugar level.

The drinker is now in the same situation as the diabetic patient who has taken too much insulin: he is suffering from hypoglycaemia – *i.e.* too low a level of blood sugar – with all its dangerous ill effects. He sweats, staggers and shakes; his intellect becomes even more blunted and he may even pass out. While this is a dangerous situation for anyone to be in, it can be lethal for some. For example, children who are very insulin-sensitive may even die from hypoglycaemia induced by alcohol.

As an evening's drinking continues, the party-goer's friends will have been able to observe the effect of alcohol on someone else's behaviour. A couple of drinks will put up the number of milligrams (mg) of alcohol per 100 millilitres (ml) of blood to 30mg per 100ml.

At this level, unless he is unusually tense and edgy, the drinker will still be in full possession of all his faculties; in many countries, he would still be able to drive legally. He will be relaxed rather than edgy, and won't be over-exuberant. With another 20mg of alcohol per 100ml of blood — say an extra pint and a half of average-strength beer — he will then have a reading of 50mg per 100ml of blood. At this level, relaxation is beginning to turn into elation and those not used to alcohol may show signs of losing inhibitions. They may be beginning to become amorous, their jokes rather more questionable, their language no longer fit for old aunts.

After ten drinks, perhaps accompanied by one drink before dinner, judgement is failing, and the voice with which the drinker is now laying down the law is becoming slurred. Someone who is by nature kindly and soft-hearted may even become maudlin and tearful. Certainly by now the over-tense person will be beginning to cause trouble, so that his friends will be trying either to edge away or, if they are kind, to persuade him or her that it is time to go home. It only requires another couple of drinks for the drinker's vision to begin to blur and for walking to degenerate into a stagger.

Twelve drinks and the drinker is out of it. He may have lost intellectual control, may be burbling on and is no longer certain where he is. People are perhaps beginning to feel that they should guide him to the taxi rank and tell the taxi driver where their passenger should be dropped.

Double this amount so that the alcohol level is at about 400mg per millilitre, and the Royal College of Physicians suggests that the drinker is no longer a drinker but a patient. He will be comatose or near comatose, and those who are not accustomed to alcohol may not come round. A few more drinks and most people won't wake up to recover from their hangover.

When should someone seek medical advice? My own view is that as soon as the patient – formerly known as 'the drinker' – has lost consciousness, no one can afford to leave him in the road. He needs to go hospital, have his stomach emptied and be where skilled help is available. Before the stomach has been emptied he may at any time be sick and inhale his vomit: a common cause of death in those who have drunk too much. Others die because they have suffered from acute alcohol poisoning, and the centres in the brain that control such essential reflex systems as respiration have been knocked out.

'Wine is a thing marvellously suited to man if, in health as in sickness, it is administered appropriately, and in just measure in accordance with the individual constitution.'

HIPPOCRATES

Holding Your Drink

Everyone's ability to drink alcohol without showing the symptoms of intoxication varies. There are rules. Men can usually drink more than women; they also become drunk more slowly and sober up faster. This doesn't show any great toughness, moral or physical superiority. It is only the result of different hormones and a different way in which alcohol is broken down in the body. Practice may not make perfect, but the drinker – whether man or woman – develops some tolerance to alcohol so that the seasoned drinker is able to take a third more than the novice.

The amount of alcohol someone can drink without becoming drunk varies from person to person. This is quite different from the amount someone can drink before getting a hangover. Drunkenness is dependent only on an individual's capacity and the amount of alcohol consumed. The hangover depends on such factors as the type of drink, the experience of the drinker, the amount drunk, the person's age and sex as well as an unexpected factor – the drinker's mood.

If drinkers are feeling optimistic, full of the joys of spring and confident, they may well avoid the hangover they deserve. On the other hand, if they are depressed and downcast when they start drinking, they may only have had a few drinks all evening, but the next morning they may have a hangover that will upset their physique as well as deepening their gloom.

The amount of alcohol drunk is obviously also of major importance, as is the gender, stature, and the race of the drinker; likewise the nature of the drink that contains the alcohol is relevant.

It was once thought that a hardened drinker, provided that his or her liver was still intact, could drink a quarter more than an average drinker. Recent research has shown that this is, in fact, an underestimate. Regular drinkers can drink *a third* more than their more abstemious neighbours. This is because they have acquired a high level of tolerance.

Although the severity of a hangover is inevitably mainly dependent on the amount of alcohol consumed, it is also determined by the amount of what are known as congeners in the drink concerned. Congeners are the natural organic chemicals that give any drink its distinctive taste, colour and smell. They make the drinks interesting, but when taken in excess, they are partly responsible for the splitting headache, the sweating skin, nausea and vomiting and the upset guts that constitute a hangover. Dehydration and a low blood-sugar level account for most of the other symptoms.

Spirits

The simple rule is that the paler the drink, the less likely it is to carry a knockout load of tasty but devastating congeners. Vodka is therefore less likely to give rise to the worst hangover you have ever had than is whisky. Too much brandy, darker than whisky, can produce an unforgettable headache. Pale rums are less hangover-producing than dark ones – one of the good reasons why Bacardi is so popular. Vodka and gin are less hangover-producing than whisky and brandy, but there are other less commonly drunk spirits such as absinthe, sambuca or pisco, which, although comparatively clear, will produce a head that will throb all day.

Gin has more congeners than vodka, but as would be expected from its clarity, less than whisky. Even among whiskies there are differences. Some pale single malts are almost as kind to drinkers as gin. But beware the home-distilled, very pale whisky that can still be found in the Highlands: its alcohol content is so great that colour becomes immaterial. In this case, it isn't the congeners it contains, but the amount of alcohol in each small tot.

Wines

Similarly, red wines, better though they are for us in the long term than white ones, give rise to a worse hangover. The darker the red wine, the more likely there is to be a hangover if drunk in excess. Burgundy, therefore, has to be treated with more care than claret. Rosé wines are made in different ways, but in general their hangover-producing potential is greater than white wines and less than reds.

Elderly vicars' wives ask for a glass of sherry, thinking they're displaying both their good breeding and their upright behaviour. No strong drinks for them. How wrong they are! Sherry is a fortified wine; the wine has been alloyed with brandy, and it will have both the kick of the brandy and the hangover that goes with a dark drink rich in congeners. Those younger people who don't think sherry too unfashionable to order often explain that they don't drink it because they find it 'liverish'. What they are really describing is a hangover they have had at some time or another. They were probably foolish enough to drink too much sherry and didn't like to admit they would have had the same symptoms from drinking an equal amount of any other drink that is as strong and loaded with congeners.

Port gives rise to the same problems, but the problems are worse. It is an even darker drink, and the hangover from it can be even greater than it would have been if they had overdone the sherry. Many people even find that dark beers cause greater hangovers than the lighter ones, even though their alcohol content may be the same.

Of course, everyone can think of exceptions to the dark-versus-light rule. Some white wines may be so badly made and disgusting to drink that even those who are sensible enough to stay sober while drinking them may regret them the next morning. The rule at any official function where the organization giving the party may have saved on the quality of the wine is to go for the cheap red rather than the cheap white.

The likelihood of a severe hangover is not only dependent on the colour of the wine, but as the municipal party may show, on its calibre. The better the wine, the less the hangover. Fine wines that have been well-made may have plenty of organic congeners that give them their flavour, but they are spared the chemicals, such as the preservative sulphur dioxide, that are now a feature of modern winemaking.

Fizzy wines are interesting. It is thought that the fizz in Champagne enables it to be absorbed more rapidly from the stomach. The faster it is absorbed, the greater the effect on mood and the quicker the alcohol induces feelings of *joie de vivre*.

Fizz is indeed more quickly absorbed than many still wines or spirits, but this is because it is deceptively bland. As it happens, the alcohol content of Champagne is as high as many still wines. How it achieves its lightening-fast intoxicating effect is mainly because its deceptive blandness doesn't cause the pylorus, the outlet of the stomach, to go into spasm, as most strong drink does. Champagne is therefore able to slip through an open gateway into the gut, where it is absorbed more quickly. Conversely, present the stomach wall with a slug of whisky and the pylorus goes into spasm, the outlet to the stomach is restricted, the alcohol stays in the stomach, where it is relatively more slowly absorbed.

Women and Drinking

For most men, the equality and emancipation of women has increased the pleasure and enjoyment of an evening's drinking. Unfortunately, welcome as women are at the bar nowadays, nature has been cruelly unfair and hasn't designed them for drinking as much as their male companions.

The absorption of alcohol is dependent on many factors: whether people have eaten before they started drinking; the nature of the drink; their individual experience of drinking; and their gender. Women have been deprived of one of the lesser enzyme systems that men are endowed with which allows the latter to deal with alcohol more efficiently. Even more unfortunately, women only have half as much of the principal enzyme involved, alcohol dehydrogenase (ADH), in the stomach as men do.

Because alcohol drunk by women is metabolized poorly in their stomachs, it goes through into the small intestine, and from there to the liver, where any that is not immediately metabolized gets into the bloodstream and hence the central nervous system. This makes women far more susceptible to getting drunk more rapidly than men. If they become drunk faster than men it isn't because they are poor, feeble creatures, but merely because the physical constitution that has given them their femininity has also made them more vulnerable to drinking.

Furthermore, the speed at which a woman is able to metabolize alcohol and thereby reduce the blood alcohol level is dependent on the stage of her monthly cycle. When a period is due, she will become drunk more readily, and will have a worse hangover the next day. Age is thus also more important for women, and much less so for men. After the menopause, women begin to develop a distribution of ADH between the liver and the stomach that is more similar to that of men. A post-menopausal woman who, when she was younger, could only have had one drink with impunity for every two her male companions enjoyed, may, in the second half of her adult life, share the bottle fifty-fifty.

Women may also be at a disadvantage when compared to men because they are usually smaller, and a greater proportion of their weight is carried as fat rather than muscle and bone. Fat is poorly supplied with blood vessels, so that the alcohol that reaches the bloodstream in women is rapidly distributed to those organs where it produces the effects of drunkenness.

It's not only women's stature that is important in the alcohol-drinking stakes. Although there are individuals to whom this doesn't apply, as a general rule, tall, muscular people — whatever their gender — can drink more than short, fat people of the same sex.

There is an exception to this. The drinker who has drunk so much that his or her liver tissue has been infiltrated by fat and later destroyed by cirrhosis will be unable to metabolize alcohol effectively or quickly. Thus, the old soak, however tall, with the beer belly and the skinny limbs, is going to be in trouble if he or she has more than a drink or two.

How Genes Affect Hangovers

Not all the peoples of the world have livers that have developed equally well to deal with alcohol; the nature of the ADH enzyme varies according to the racial origins of the drinker. Those from some Far Eastern countries have a form of ADH that metabolizes alcohol with difficulty, so that the slightly different enzyme systems they have produce different chemicals than are found in Europeans.

One of the most obvious examples of this is the excessive flushing that occurs in people from the Far East after they have been drinking. It is said that, even so, their hangover is no worse than that experienced by most Europeans. However hard they try to keep their alcohol consumption down, the flushing it causes demonstrates that they have been drinking. There is no pretending to their husbands or wives that they have been working late at the office, for a scarlet and perspiring face is there for everyone to see.

Another, but less well-known, example of a racial difference is that which affects twenty-five percent of people of Jewish extraction. This minority of Jewish people also have a different ADH enzyme system from most of those in the Western world and don't metabolize alcohol as easily and efficiently as their fellow British or French citizens. Whereas those from the Far East always claim that their hangovers are no worse than Westerners, those who carry this Jewish gene are more likely to suffer from a serious hangover after a smaller quantity of alcohol than do their gentile neighbours. However, they don't suffer from the same degree of post-alcohol flushing as do some other nationalities.

The ability to drink alcohol without suffering serious physical and social consequences varies from race to race. In the Western world, alcohol has been drunk for 10,000 years so that natural selection has determined that those who have neither physical nor mental resistance are less likely to have survived to have children of their own. The metabolism of many people from the Far East, and indeed, some of Native Americans, breaks down alcohol in a different way to those in the West. The chemicals that are produced while it is being metabolized in these races have unpleasant side effects.

Eating to Avoid a Hangover

The most avaricious bar owners make certain that there are not many chairs in the bar. They know that when people are standing they drink more. They will pretend that they don't have chairs because they want a jolly party atmosphere. The jolly party atmosphere has little to do with whether a group of drinkers are standing or sitting except that those who sit drink more slowly. Those who sit in a bar are able to rest their drinks on a table, whereas those who stand with a drink in their hands drink faster – their bills will be correspondingly larger, and the noise they make greater.

There is another disadvantage to standing while drinking. Those who have a comfortable chair and a table in front of them are more likely to consume sandwiches, canapés or simply crisps and nuts. The point is that they are eating when they're drinking. The popular theory – which happens to be correct but incomplete – is that eating delays the absorption of the alcohol. This is particularly true if there is some fat in the food, even if it is only in the crisps or smoked salmon.

Fat triggers the release of a hormone from the stomach wall that delays stomach emptying. As a result, alcohol remains in the stomach longer, where it is absorbed slowly, and it isn't rapidly emptied into the small intestine, where it is absorbed quickly. The faster the alcohol is absorbed, the more likely a person is to become drunk, and the worse the hangover will be the next day.

Even better than having bar food with the evening's drinks is to take precautionary measures before setting out. The traditional preparation for a night out is to drink milk. Milk is ideal, because it contains fat which produces the hormone that delays stomach emptying; contrary to popular belief, however, it doesn't 'coat' the inside of the stomach. Any food will have a similar but lesser effect.

Some carbohydrates are rapidly digested both by saliva and the gastric juices, so any snacks eaten at home before leaving for a party should preferably contain both protein and fat. It is the butter and the ham in the sandwich, rather than the bread, that will prevent drunkenness later. Having a few slices of dry

'Who drinks one bowl hath scant delight; to poorest passion he was born; who drains the score must e'er expect to rue the headache of the morn.'

RICHARD BURTON

The Stages of Drunkenness

Stages of drunkenness have been measured differently by different authorities over the years. Doctors have traditionally learned them by reference to something called 'The Rules of D'.

The first stage of drinking leaves drinkers 'Dry and Decent'. After a few more drinks, they become 'Delighted and Devilish'. Continue drinking and they are 'Delinquent and Disgusting'. As they begin to lose their coordination and senses, they become 'Dizzy and Delirious' before becoming 'Dazed and Dejected', and finally, 'Dead Drunk'.

In contrast, an older generation of doctors who had had a classical education used to plot the evening's drinking in terms of the 'Six Oses'. Initially drinkers became 'Verbose', then 'Amorous'; after this 'Grandiose' and then, when the rot sets in, they are 'Morose' becoming 'Lachrymose' (or 'tearful', for those who don't know) and finally, 'Comatose'.

Hangover Cures from the Past

The hangover cures that were popularized from the 1990s onwards have always relied, perhaps unknowingly, on the scientific principles of reducing gastro-intestinal inflammation and restoring the fluid balance and blood sugar levels. Not so further back in history. Ancient hangover cures were altogether more exciting and exotic. The Romans, for example, enjoyed drinking so much that laws were introduced to control the number who could party together. They thus also developed a number of special hangover cures.

Today's drinker who is hoping for a Bloody Mary would look askance at the Romans' cure of two raw owl eggs, and would throw up if confronted by owl's eyes. Yet both cures were advocated by the naturalist and philosopher Pliny the Elder, who also recommended sheep's lungs. An ancient Assyrian remedy also favoured by the Romans involved mixing ground swallow's beak with a teaspoon of myrrh. If that didn't work, another customary pick-me-up was a broth made of cloves and water. The Roman politician Cato swore by a bowl of stewed cabbage topped with raw almonds. Other Roman remedies included roasted boar's lung and powdered pumice stone to soothe aching heads and sore stomachs.

By the Middle Ages, the emphasis had moved on to fish. One recipe, for instance, recommends downing an eel with chopped bitter almonds. The premise, at least, was sound; to this day, a high-protein breakfast (for those who have the stomach for it) works wonders. It restores the blood-sugar levels and the protein ensures that this amount of circulating sugar, once the level has recovered, remains at a point where the shakes will be eased, the headache relieved, the sweating reduced and the nausea settled.

In colonial times, the cure for over-indulgence was flogging and bleeding with leeches.

Meanwhile, in China, people used to put a round, flat stone under the sufferer's tongue. It might be said that it achieved the desired effect since, perhaps unsurprisingly, it made the hangover sufferer even sicker than he was already...

In Mexico, a bowl of tripe, hominy, and calves feet was given to those suffering from a hangover.

Of course, individuals have always devised their own remedies, and not all of them are sympathetic. It is well-known, for example, that former Soviet leader Nikita Khrushchev would often taunt a friend suffering from a hangover by whispering into his ear: 'There's only one cure for what ails you.' As a glint of hope appeared in his friend's eyes, Khrushchev would then hoot with laughter and shout: 'Death!'

Notorious boozer W. C. Fields was a little less cruel and a bit more straightforward: 'Fill a tall glass and drink till dizzy.'

Fields was actually on the right track. The majority of hangover cures throughout history have included some form of alcohol in the recipe. This is based on sound medical logic. There is, however, a distinction (albeit minor) between those potions created especially to serve a predetermined medical need and the alcohol-based cures constructed from instinct rather than from methodology. For over four centuries the latter group has been known by the rubric 'hair of the dog', and you will find a good selection of these, starting on page 49.

How to Relieve a Hangover

The real way to deal with a hangover is to deal with each of its constituent parts. The first measures to take are those that deal with dehydration and hypo-glycaemia. The hungover drinker should take several cups or glasses of sweet tea or fruit juices. Coffee has an undeserved reputation as a hangover cure. Although coffee is a fluid, it is also a diuretic, so it increases fluid lost through the kidneys — hence fruit juices are a better choice as a rehydrating agent. Coffee does have one advantage, however. If the night has been restless and sleep has been in short supply, the caffeine serves to wake the hungover person up, and to keep the intellect alert.

When the drinker returns home, there will still be signs of drunkenness, but the only signs of the hangover that is to come are a mild headache and nausea. The immediate first-aid, and the appropriate prophylactic, is to drink two or three glasses of water. This will ease the dehydration that is already beginning to affect the body. By this time the drinker will have noticed that as he or she has been drinking, the alcohol has had a diuretic effect. The kidneys will excrete more fluid, and trips to the bathroom will have become more frequent and more urgent.

Once in bed, the heavy drinker will probably fall asleep quite readily – provided he's not suffering from the drinker's dread: pillow-spin (also known in some circles as 'whirly-beds'). Pillow-spin is the result of the cerebellum and the organs of balance in the ear being upset by the neurotoxic properties of even the finest claret.

Everyone has a favourite way of dealing with pillow-spin. The majority verdict is that the light should be left on, and the pillows should be propped against the bed-head so that the drinker can lie back against them (just like in hospital). The drinker should rest with the eyes open, hoping to drop off to sleep before having to rush to the loo to be sick – just in the same way as a bad sailor has to make for the rails around the ship's deck once the swell increases.

Fortunately, drunken people are partially anaesthetized by alcohol. In a few hours, as the anaesthetic effect of the alcohol begins to wear off, they are in danger of suffering an alcoholic's 'false dawn'. If this happens, the drinker will wake in the early hours of the morning, drenched in sweat. The sweating is the result of hypoglycaemia, whereas the wakefulness stems from the nerve damage to the brain cells.

Next morning, after a restless few hours between the false dawn and the real time to get up, the hangover will have moved on. The headache will now be reaching its peak, the nausea will be incapacitating, and life will hardly seem worth living.

Later in the day, if the hangover is really severe, the headache and other, more subtle changes to the brain make constructive thought impossible. Initially, hungover people are usually too dejected to be surly and aggressive, but even if their tempers are not inflamed, their stomach and guts are. After a bad night and a serious hangover, it is not a question of not wanting food but of not being able to bear food in any form.

Food is just something that can't even be thought about without fear of it triggering another bout of nausea. Drinkers' guts are no happier than their stomachs, and the hungover won't want to move far from the bathroom for several hours. As they begin to sober up, they regain enough initiative to become irritable and fractious. Even if left untreated (or badly treated), all but the worst hangover should be gone by teatime. The drinker will be able to have – if not enjoy – a light supper.

It is important that any hypoglycaemia should be treated without causing such an insulin response that there is a rebound reduction in blood sugar. This is achieved by having a hearty breakfast of porridge (the carbohydrates in porridge have a low glycaemic index as they are in the form of polysaccharide: a slowly absorbable sugar), and similarly, the protein in the bacon and eggs slowly but persistently corrects blood-sugar levels.

The headache should ease once the blood sugar has been corrected, and soluble analgesics such as paracetamol will hasten it on its way, but they shouldn't be taken in any great quantity. Too much soluble aspirin may further inflame the stomach; paracetamol in excess is toxic to the liver – and the liver has already had a very difficult night.

The Importance of Vitamins

The heavy drinker who is thin and undernourished is in even greater danger than the one who is overweight and malnourished. All those who drink to excess are likely to suffer from vitamin deficiency. Vitamins are the little-thought-about constituents of the diet that are essential for healthy living.

Drinkers must compensate for a diet that is likely to be poor in vitamins, and for a digestive system that only inadequately absorbs what vitamins there are. Thus, while drinkers need more vitamins than the rest of the population, they usually have less.

The drinking person's diet should contain additional vitamin A, vitamin B_1, vitamin B_{12}, vitamin C, vitamin D and folic acid. Without adequate supplies of vitamin A, a drinker will suffer poor vision, skin diseases and will have a reduced resistance to infection.

The recommended daily dose is not more than 7,500 micrograms for women and 9,000 micrograms for men. After the drinking is over — or even while it is still continuing — the drinker should try and have as much liver, milk, butter, cheese, eggs and oily fish as possible. The vegetables he chooses should be the highly coloured ones. Forget the lettuce; go for the dark-green vegetables such as broccoli, spinach and green peppers. Coloured fruits and vegetables are rich in betacarotene, from which vitamin A is made by the body. Carrots, red peppers, chillies and tomatoes are all good sources.

Vitamin C is usually in short supply in heavy drinkers. Without it, wounds heal badly, gums bleed, resistance to infection is lowered and scurvy may ensue. Fresh fruit such as blackcurrants, strawberries, kiwi fruit, oranges and grapefruit are good sources, as are peppers on the vegetable front. Salads are also excellent supplies of vitamin C, and most fresh garden produce provides a ready supply.

Heavy drinkers are also usually short of vitamins from the B group. Fish, liver, eggs, yeast extracts, grains, nuts and cereals provide a mixed source of the B vitamins. Extra quantities of vitamin B are needed by those who are stressed, ill or who smoke. Folic acid is also essential.

Drinking is a Pleasure

There can be few better summaries of the advantages of
drinking than that made by a Frenchman when speaking
about Champagne:

> *No government could survive without Champagne.*
> *Champagne in the throats of our diplomatic people*
> *is like oil in the wheels of an engine. Burgundies*
> *for kings, Champagne for duchesses and claret*
> *for gentlemen.*

He could have added, had he been alive today, that all
forms of alcohol – not just, but including, these aristo-
cratic drinks – now serve a similar function in ninety
percent of households of the Western world. The
majority of drinkers suffer the occasional hangover
when younger, but only a few suffer from the ill effects
of long-term drinking.

Alcohol still oils the wheels of diplomatic occasions,
as well as practically every other form of social
gathering. A wedding without alcohol is a rarity. It is

there when a child is christened and served after someone dies. It loosens the atmosphere at every party and is an integral part of daily life.

Relatively very few people become alcoholics. The trick is to avoid regularly drinking to excess, or drinking too much on one occasion if it is going to interfere with driving, working machinery or making important decisions. Inevitably, doctors, who only see the ill and not the fit, and the police, who only deal with the delinquent and not the well-behaved, naturally develop an unfavourable opinion of drinking.

Although these aspects of drinking need to be understood so that they may be guarded against, they shouldn't deter the ordinary person from enjoying a bottle of wine at home or two or three drinks in the Adam & Eve or George & Dragon.

'I pray thee, let me and my
fellow have a Haire of the dog
that bit us last night…'

JOHN HEYWOOD
1546

Hair of the Dog Cures

In ancient Greek and Roman medicine, the principle that 'like cures like' meant that if something had caused trouble, a small quantity of it was incorporated into the cure. For this reason it was usual for the dressing applied to a dog bite to contain a sample of hair from the dog that had bitten the person. This same principle still exists in the realm of alcoholic hangover cures, so that if someone has made themselves ill through drinking alcohol, the cure also contains alcohol.

Apple of My Eye

In the Southern states of America, after a heavy evening and a hard day's work, there is nothing more relaxing than to mix a drink of fresh apple juice laced with Bourbon. The ravages of the previous night, and the stresses of the day, are forgotten once the Bourbon has revived flagging spirits and the apple has restored vitamin levels and provided a few calories. Mint adds just the freshness that a jaded mouth needs.

6 apples
mint leaves, to taste
60ml or 2 fl oz Bourbon

Core and peel the apples. Place them in a blender or a juicer. Add ice to the juice and mix in the Bourbon.

The Apothecary

Herbs have almost magical qualities, but it requires a skilled apothecary to recognize these. Luckily, many herbal-based spirits are available that overcome this problem. This recipe, frequently recommended by Salvatore Calabrese, formerly of The Lanesborough Hotel in London and now at 50 St James, could have been designed to restore the equilibrium of your stomach. After the herbal-rich Italian Punt e Mes and Fernet Branca combine with crème de menthe, you will be able to face the world.

 30ml or 1 fl oz Fernet Branca
 30ml or 1 fl oz white crème de menthe
 30ml or 1 fl oz Punt e Mes

Pour all ingredients into a mixing glass filled with ice. Stir. Strain into a cocktail glass.

The man who has not been drunk
does not know the value of sobriety.

CHINESE PROVERB

The Assassin

This isn't so much 'hair of the dog' but most of its coat. Even so, Johnny Buffa, bartender at Big Al's topless nightclub in San Francisco, made it famous in the Sixties, and The Assassin became a national institution. There are a few calories with it, but you might feel even better if you also had a long, cool drink of fruit juice.

> 10ml or ⅓ fl oz white crème de menthe
> around 7.5ml or ¼ fl oz Fernet Branca
> 30ml or 1 fl oz port

Mix together all the ingredients and serve in an old-fashioned glass without ice.

Aura

Luciano Fierabracci of The Ground Floor, New York, recommends a three-stage treatment the morning after that will leave you in a fit state to enjoy lunch.

*

Start at 7AM with a light breakfast of nothing more demanding than honey and milk. The milk rehydrates and the honey provides rapidly absorbable sugar.

> *60ml or 2 fl oz milk*
> *2 tablespoons honey*

Stir to boiling point in a saucepan. Pour into a mug and drink as hot as you can.

*

If you're strong enough to go to work, a tot of rum at about 9AM, after you're at your desk, will give you the energy to face another day. The recipe provides much-needed fluid and sugar.

freshly squeezed juice of 1 orange
freshly squeezed juice of half a lemon
30ml or 1 fl oz light rum

Stir to boiling in a saucepan. Serve in a heat-proof glass.

✻

The third stage of the Aura is a modified coffee break. By
11AM, you're already feeling more chirpy, you may even be
better company and able to smile at your colleagues.
Death before lunch no longer seems a possibility.

15ml or ½ fl oz Campari
30ml or 1 fl oz vodka
90ml or 3 fl oz tomato juice
15ml or ½ fl oz freshly squeezed lemon juice
3 dashes Worcestershire sauce

Pour all ingredients into a shaker filled with ice and
shake. Strain into a highball glass filled with ice.

Back to Work

This hangover cure is recommended by Francis Ane, head bartender at the Orly Hilton in Orly, France. It contains some spirits, some refreshing, vitamin-rich lemon, and tomato juice packed with lycopene, a strong antioxidant. The Tabasco will sharpen a jaded tongue and mouth. This potion should be followed by a long, cool glass of water.

Juice of 1 lemon
45ml or 1 ½ oz Bourbon or rye whiskey
30ml or 1 fl oz tomato juice
1 dash Tabasco sauce

Shake all ingredients together and serve in a highball glass with lots of ice.

Baltimore Eggnog

Eggnogs epitomize the Thirties. The classic combination of alcohol (to settle the stomach) and cream, egg and milk to maintain blood-sugar levels works. This drink was once popular during any festive period, but nowadays, it is mainly associated with Christmas.

30ml or 1 fl oz brandy
30ml or 1 fl oz Madeira
20ml or about ⅔ fl oz dark rum
1 tablespoon gommé syrup
1 free-range egg
20ml or about ⅔ fl oz heavy (double) cream
90ml or 3 fl oz milk

Pour all ingredients into a shaker filled with ice. Shake well. Strain into a highball glass filled with ice. Grate fresh nutmeg over the top.

Banana Cow

This recipe comes from the famous Trader Vic's restaurant group, and this version was introduced in Beverly Hills in the Sixties by barman Chris Papajohn. He swore by it and claimed it was the best hangover cure ever served. He gave it a curious recommendation: that it was just like taking a cold shower. This might have put many drinkers off, but it has remained popular.

30ml or 1 fl oz white rum
1 whole ripe banana
90ml or 3 fl oz milk
dash Angostura bitters
dash vanilla essence
1 teaspoon caster sugar

Pour all the ingredients into a blender and blend for ten seconds. Add half a scoop of crushed ice and blend again until smooth. Serve in a goblet.

Batonnet

Some people find that one of the most tiresome consequences of drinking is that it can destroy sleep. If you
ever feel tired the next morning, Colin Peter Field, the
bartender at Bar Hemingway in the Ritz Hotel, Paris,
has the answer. He recommends that customers who
lack energy the morning after should try a great reviver
like Cognac, combined with tonic and white wine.

30ml or 1 fl oz Cognac
90ml or 3 fl oz white wine
two cinnamon sticks
tonic water

Pour the Cognac and white wine into a tumbler filled
with ice. Break the cinnamon sticks and drop them into
the glass. Top up with tonic.

Black Velvet

There can be few serious drinkers who haven't lunched on a Sunday by having a couple of Black Velvets. Yet just in case you haven't discovered its restorative powers, here is the recipe. Combining Champagne and Guinness was an idea that started at Brook's Club in 1861, and is said to have been created by the barman who felt that, because Prince Albert had died, a black drink was in order.

½ glass chilled Guinness
½ glass chilled dry Champagne

Combine both ingredients in a tankard. Sip slowly. Feel revived.

Blood Transfusion

The alcohol provides the hair of the dog for your stomach, the Fernet Branca wakes you up, and the calories restore some blood-sugar levels. It is a long drink, so helps with rehydration. The combination is said to be either a kill or cure.

30ml or 1 fl oz vodka
30ml or 1 fl oz sherry
30ml or 1 fl oz Fernet Branca
150ml or 5 fl oz tomato juice
30ml or 1 fl oz fresh lime juice
pinch celery salt
2 dashes Worcestershire sauce

Fill a highball glass with ice-cubes. Pour the vodka and sherry over the ice first, then add the tomato and lime juice, then the celery salt and Worcestershire sauce. Stir. Float a layer of Fernet Branca on top.

Bloody Bull

The Bloody Bull has been chasing hangovers for years. It wouldn't have lasted unless it was successful as well as simple. It is a combination of a Bullshot and a Bloody Mary, and is said to be better than either of the two used singly.

30ml or 1 fl oz vodka
60ml or 2 fl oz beef bouillon
60ml or 2 fl oz tomato juice
30ml or 1 fl oz fresh lemon juice
2 dashes Worcestershire sauce
pinch celery salt

Pour all ingredients into a cocktail shaker filled with ice. Shake. Strain into a highball glass filled with ice.

Bloody Caesar

Tony Bennett is still crooning, and this drink, created for him at Caesar's Palace in Las Vegas, is still being taken for hangovers. It was originally mixed to revive and invigorate the singer when he had to recover between performances.

30ml or 1 fl oz vodka
150ml or 5 fl oz Clamato
(a mixture of tomato and clam juice)
20ml or about ⅔ fl oz fresh lemon juice
pinch celery salt
dash Tabasco sauce
2 dashes Worcestershire sauce
freshly ground black pepper

Pour the Clamato and lemon juice into a highball glass filled with ice. Add the vodka and other ingredients. Stir. Garnish with a wedge of lime on the rim. Serve with a stirrer.

Bloody Maria

This recipe is another great classic. It is closely related to a Bloody Mary, but rather than vodka, it is made with tequila. Working on the principle of the hair of the dog, it is particularly useful for those who have overdone the Tequila the night before.

> 30ml or 1 fl oz Tequila
> 150ml or 5 fl oz tomato juice
> dash fresh lemon juice
> pinch celery salt
> pinch black pepper
> 4 dashes Tabasco sauce
> 4 dashes Worcestershire sauce

Pour all ingredients into a cocktail shaker filled with ice. Shake. Strain into a highball glass filled with ice. Garnish with a celery stick and a wedge of lime.

Bloody Mary

The Bloody Mary is arguably the most popular pick-me-up for hangovers in the world. Few adults have never had one, and no one who has a hangover can have failed to try its magical effects. Its origins are uncertain, but the two most favoured claimants are barmen in Harry's New York Bar in Paris and at the St Regis bar in New York.

The barman at the latter hotel claimed that the combination of vodka and tomato juice was a favourite of the Astor family, and that he revived it some years after Jacob Astor went down on the *Titanic*. According to the rest of the story, he spiced up the Astor recipe with a dash of Worcestershire sauce, and the Bloody Mary was created, although it was initially known as the Red Snapper (*see* page 123).

Whatever its origins, the recipe for the classic Bloody Mary follows on page 72.

Bloody Mary, continued

    30ml or 1 fl oz vodka
    150ml or 5 fl oz tomato juice
    20ml or about ⅔ fl oz fresh lemon juice
    pinch celery salt
    2 dashes Worcestershire sauce
    2 dashes Tabasco sauce
    freshly ground black pepper
    celery stalk (optional)

Fill a highball glass with ice-cubes, then pour in the tomato and lemon juices. Add the vodka. Add the other items and stir. Add a quick grinding of black pepper. Garnish with a wedge of lime on the rim, and a stalk of celery, if requested. Serve with a stirrer.

Bloody Swedish Blonde

Another Calabrese creation. The bartender discovered that some of his Scandinavian customers found that the combination of ingredients in this drink calms the nerves, even as it tops up their supplies of minerals and vitamins.

> 30ml or 1 fl oz akvavit
> 125ml or 4 fl oz tomato juice
> pinch ground toasted fennel seed
> 20ml or about ⅔ fl oz fresh lemon juice
> large pinch caraway seed
> lemon twist
> salt and pepper, to taste

Combine the akvavit, tomato juice and fennel seed in a mixing glass and swirl it around gently. Strain into a highball glass filled with ice-cubes. Add the lemon juice. Garnish with caraway seeds and a twist of lemon. Serve with a stirrer.

Boston Flip

Eggnogs may have been popularized in the Thirties, but similar drinks were being made in the seventeenth century. They contained beaten eggs, alcohol, spices and sugar. The Boston Flip used to be stirred by pouring the cocktail backwards and forwards between two containers until it was of a smooth consistency, then heated by putting a hot poker in the mixture before serving it. It is no longer served as a long drink, and is served cold. Nutmeg is usually sprinkled over it. For those who don't like rum or Bourbon, other spirits may be substituted.

30ml or 1 fl oz Bourbon
30ml or 1 fl oz Madeira
1 free-range egg yolk
dash gommé syrup

Pour all ingredients into a cocktail shaker filled with ice. Shake well. Strain into a goblet. Garnish with grated nutmeg.

Bourbon Pick-Me-Up

The Bourbon Pick-Me-Up is especially recommended by those who have drunk too much Bourbon the night before. Ben Reed, former barman at the Met Bar in London, suggests making it with fresh mint, combined with Branca Menta and Bourbon.

> *30ml or 1 fl oz Bourbon*
> *20ml or about ⅔ fl oz Branca Menta*
> *20ml or about ⅔ fl oz fresh lemon juice*
> *8 fresh mint leaves*

Pour all the ingredients into a cocktail shaker filled with ice. Shake. Strain into an old-fashioned glass filled with ice. Garnish with a sprig of fresh mint.

'Only Irish Coffee provides in a single glass all four essential food groups: alcohol, caffeine, sugar, fat.'

ALEX LEVINE

Brandy Flip

A simple flip made from egg yolk combined with brandy. As mentioned earlier, however, flips can be made with any other spirit. The sugar restores the blood-sugar level and the fat in the egg ensures that it doesn't fall again as soon as the drink is downed.

30ml or 1 fl oz brandy
1 whole free-range egg
2 teaspoons castor sugar
grating of fresh nutmeg

Pour all the ingredients into a cocktail shaker filled with ice. Shake and strain into a wine glass. Grate fresh nutmeg over the top.

Breakfast Eggnog

Here's a slightly more complicated eggnog. As with all 'nogs, this one is rich in fat and protein, as well as sugar to correct the blood-sugar level and alcohol to provide the hair of the dog and a bit of a lift. The milk has an alkaline effect on the acid being secreted by an irritated stomach. All in all, this is a good mixture, easily taken by those who can't face bacon and eggs and fruit juice.

> *1 fresh free-range egg*
> *30ml or 1 fl oz orange Curaçao*
> *30ml or 1 fl oz brandy*
> *150ml or 5 fl oz milk*
> *grating of fresh nutmeg*

Pour all ingredients, except the milk, into a cocktail shaker filled with ice. Shake. Strain into a highball glass and add the milk. Stir. Sprinkle freshly grated nutmeg over the top.

Buck's Fizz

Like the Bloody Mary, Black Velvet and Bullshot, the Buck's Fizz is to cocktail drinkers what mince pies are to Christmas. It was devised by Mr McGarry, the barman at the Buck's Club, London, in 1921. He was always insistent that it should be two-thirds Champagne to one-third fresh orange juice, and was greatly aggrieved when drinkers tried their own versions and described it as a Buck's Fizz.

fresh orange juice
Champagne

The size of the Champagne glass dictates how much of the above you will use. Follow McGarry's two-thirds Champagne to one-third orange juice measurements and stir gently.

Bullshot

Bangkok is famous for many delights, but few know that this is where the Bullshot originated. Created by Axel Gorlach at the Rama Hotel, this hangover cocktail rapidly became world-famous. Some people recommend it instead of lunch; others serve it instead of soup, and countless hangover sufferers have drunk it medicinally.

It owes its name to the presence of beef bouillon – an essential, but not overpowering, part of the recipe. The Tabasco and Worcestershire sauces provide its punch.

150ml or 5 fl oz beef bouillon or substitute

dash fresh lemon juice

celery salt

dash of Tabasco sauce

2 dashes Worcestershire sauce

30ml or 1 fl oz vodka

freshly ground black pepper

wedge of lime

Pour the bouillon, lemon juice, celery salt, Tabasco and Worcestershire sauces into a cocktail shaker filled with ice, then add the vodka. Shake. Strain into a highball glass. Add a quick grinding of black pepper. Garnish with a wedge of lime on the rim. Serve with a stirrer.

Camel

For those not fond of too much hair of dogs, F. Krikzonis at Club 17, in Athens, Greece, has devised a combination of ouzo and tomato juice. As with all pick-me-ups it should be taken early in the morning, preferably with a breakfast that includes starchy carbohydrates such as oatmeal, cereal or even toast and a large glass of orange juice.

20ml or ⅔ fl oz ouzo
90ml or about 3 fl oz soda
juice of half a lemon (if large) or 1 lemon (if small)
dash of Angostura bitters
ice

If you're still shaky two hours after drinking this mixture, try mixing an Alexandrette, which consists of ice, 1 egg white, 1 jigger Cognac, 1 jigger cream and about half a cup of coffee.

Campari Nobile

An award-winner created by Salvatore Calabrese for the 1993 Campari Barman of the Year competition. The juices are full of vitamins, and the bitter lemon is refreshing. Limoncello, from Italy's Amalfi coast, adds sunshine to your spirits.

20ml or about ⅔ fl oz vodka
20ml or about ⅔ fl oz Campari
10ml or ⅓ fl oz Limoncello
90ml or 3 fl oz combined fresh orange and raspberry juices
bitter lemon
raspberries, a mint sprig, and a twist of orange to garnish

Pour all ingredients, except the bitter lemon, into a cocktail shaker filled with ice. Shake. Strain into a highball glass filled with ice. Top up with bitter lemon. Stir. Garnish with five raspberries and a sprig of mint, plus a twist of orange on the rim. Serve with a straw and a stirrer.

'Alcohol is a very necessary article. It enables Parliament to do things at eleven at night that no sane person would do at eleven in the morning.'

GEORGE BERNARD SHAW

Cecil Pick-Me-Up

No one knows who Cecil was, but he must have been a regular drinker in a well-known American bar before Prohibition. Like many of the recipes that date from the Twenties and Thirties, this one includes the four commonly found ingredients of pick-me-ups: Champagne, egg, brandy and sugar. An enlightened twenty-first-century doctor couldn't improve on this basic mixture.

1 free-range egg yolk
30ml or 1 fl oz brandy
1 teaspoon castor sugar
Champagne

Pour all the ingredients, except the Champagne, into a cocktail shaker filled with ice. Shake. Strain into a Champagne flute. Top up with Champagne.

Champagne Cocktail

The Champagne Cocktail has been around for three generations, but is now less popular, as it packs a rougher punch than its bland taste suggests. Its alcoholic content has made it unsuitable as a cocktail if those drinking it are intending to drive, but it is still an excellent pick-me-up after a heavy night's drinking. It is said to have originated in the southern states of America, but this is only conjecture.

chilled Champagne
dash brandy
1 sugar cube
Angostura bitters
slices of orange

Place a cube of sugar in each Champagne flute and soak with the Angostura bitters. Add enough brandy to cover the sugar cube and fill the glasses with Champagne. Garnish with orange slices.

Champagne Pick-Me-Up

This variation of the Buck's Fizz would probably have shocked the barman who originally produced the Fizz. This mixture is different because it contains brandy and the proportions have been changed. The dash of lemon is said to freshen up the mixture – and with it, a stale mouth.

30ml or 1 fl oz brandy
20ml or about ⅔ fl oz fresh orange juice
20ml or about ⅔ fl oz fresh lemon juice
Champagne

Pour the first three ingredients into a cocktail shaker filled with ice. Shake. Strain into a Champagne flute. Stir. Top up with Champagne. Stir again to serve.

'Champagne is the only wine
that leaves a woman beautiful
after drinking it.'

MADAME DE POMPADOUR

'Alcohol is necessary for a man so
that he can have a good opinion of himself,
undisturbed by the facts.'

FINLEY PETER DUNNE

Corpse Reviver

Many pick-me-ups claim to have the Lazarus effect. All work on the same principle, but were created by different barmen in a variety of hotels across the world. The first version was reputed to have been introduced by Frank Meier in 1926 at the Cambon Bar of The Ritz in Paris.

1 glass Pernod
juice of a quarter lemon
Champagne

Pour the lemon juice and Pernod into a Champagne coupe over a cube of ice. Fill with Champagne. Stir slowly. Serve.

Later, the Savoy had its own version, published in 1930. To many people, this is the Corpse Reviver *par excellence*.

30ml or 1 fl oz brandy
30ml or 1 fl oz sweet vermouth
30ml or 1 fl oz Calvados

Pour all ingredients into a mixing glass filled with ice. Stir. Strain into a cocktail glass.

More recently, Johnny Johnson, a barman at the Savoy's American Bar in London, introduced another variation.

30ml or 1 fl oz brandy
30ml or 1 fl oz white crème de menthe
30ml or 1 fl oz Fernet Branca

Pour all ingredients into a mixing glass filled with ice. Stir. Strain into a cocktail glass.

Effective Cures

Elmer Keifner, head bartender at the Hotel Vancouver in Canada, modestly produced only three pick-me-ups that he described as 'effective cures'. They were designed to deal, respectively, with the symptoms of a monumental hangover, an average hangover and a bit of a hangover. They work because they contain a trace of alcohol, sugar, protein and fat. Whichever one you choose, the Effective Cure is a liquid breakfast that needs to be supplemented with a long, cool drink of orange juice.

Extremely Effective Cure (for a large hangover)

> 30ml or 1 fl oz Cognac
> 60ml or 2 fl oz dry port
> 10ml or ⅓ fl oz sugar syrup
> 1 whole egg

Pour the above into the shaker with crushed ice, shake well and strain into goblet.

Effective Cure
(for a medium hangover)

125ml or 4 fl oz hot coffee
45ml or 1½ fl oz Kahlua or other coffee liqueur

Pour into a mug and serve very hot. No sugar is needed.

The Fifty Percent Effective Cure
(for a slight hangover)

30ml or 1 fl oz Courvoisier
90ml or 3 fl oz port or Madeira

Pour into cocktail glass. No ice is necessary.

Eggnog

Another eggnog, but this one deserves mention as it has been used for four hundred years. Why it should have been considered part of some family's traditional Christmas is as uncertain as its actual origins, but the term 'noggin' is still used to describe a small glass of stronger-than-average beer or, more loosely, any strong drink that could be knocked back quickly.

1 free-range egg
30ml or 1 fl oz brandy
30ml or 1 fl oz dark rum
1 tablespoon gommé syrup
90ml or 3 fl oz milk
grating of fresh nutmeg

Pour all ingredients, except the milk, into a cocktail shaker. Shake. Strain into a goblet. Stir in the milk. Grate fresh nutmeg on top.

Eye-opener

Absinthe had a sinister reputation at the end of the nineteenth century, but modern absinthes leave eyesight unthreatened. In fact, this absinthe mixture is reputed to so strengthen the eyelids so that even the most hungover can bear to open them. The term 'eye-opener' was used in the Twenties and Thirties, so it is likely that the recipe dates from about this period.

> 2 dashes absinthe
> 2 dashes orange Curaçao
> 2 dashes crème de Noyau
> 30ml or 1 fl oz rum
> 1 teaspoon castor sugar
> 1 free-range egg yolk

Pour all the ingredients into a cocktail shaker filled with ice. Shake. Strain into a cocktail glass.

Fallen Angel

This classic gin-based cocktail would be useful after a heavy night's drinking because it contains some bland alcoholic ingredients that will soothe the stomach, and enough calories to help correct a depleted blood-sugar level. Peppermint, an essential part of crème de menthe, is a traditional remedy for an uneasy digestion.

60ml or 2 fl oz gin
dash white crème de menthe
dash Angostura bitters
dash fresh lemon juice

Pour all the ingredients into a cocktail shaker filled with ice. Shake well. Strain into a cocktail glass.

Fernet Branca Cocktail

This is another recipe that relies heavily on the power of herbs, and is a favourite remedy prescribed by many leading barmen. Fernet Branca is made in Italy and contains extracts from over forty herbs. It was first sold in 1844 by the Branca family – hence its name. Among others, the herbs include aloe vera, angelica, camomile, cinchona, (from which quinine is prepared), gentian, peppermint, saffron, rue and wormwood.

30ml or 1 fl oz Fernet Branca
30ml or 1 fl oz sweet vermouth
30ml or 1 fl oz gin

Pour all ingredients into a cocktail shaker filled with ice. Shake. Strain into a cocktail glass.

Fog Lifter

Las Vegas is no longer only a gambling city, but is now attracting tourists of all ages and from all parts of the world. Even so, it still features a multitude of bars and casinos. Those who have had a bad night gambling don't just need a pick-me-up so that they feel better, they need one that will blunt the emotions and allow them some peace of mind. This recipe, designed to lift the fog of despair, was invented by Walt Hudson at the Fabulous Flamingo Hotel.

30ml or 1 fl oz brandy
45ml or 1½ fl oz Pernod
60ml or 2 fl oz cream
1 egg

Mix all the above ingredients in a glass, and serve. Everything should seem clearer after drinking.

Gloom Chaser

This is a comparatively late pick-me-up that enjoyed popularity among the hippy generation who haunted the Tokyo Club bar in Rome, in the Sixties. Olive oil supplements the fat in the egg yolk, but like other eggnogs the brandy provides the hair of the dog, and the paprika gives it an unusual kick and enhances the Worcestershire sauce.

1 egg yolk
half a teaspoon olive oil
15ml or ½ fl oz Cognac
paprika
10 drops Worcestershire sauce

Shake all ingredients together and serve.

Hair of the Dog

P. G. Wodehouse devised a recipe that the ever-faithful and tactful Jeeves served Bertie Wooster whenever his morning was troubled by a severe hangover. Some suggest that the use of honey maintains higher blood sugar than other sugars, but actually the opposite is true. The long-term success of Jeeves's cocktail is due to the fact that the alcohol and the sugary honey are combined with cream. Cream contains fat and protein that prevent the rapid absorption of this comparatively sweet drink.

60ml or 2 fl oz Scotch
30ml or 1 fl oz double cream
1 large teaspoon clear honey

Pour all ingredients into a cocktail shaker filled with ice. Shake vigorously to let the honey infuse. Strain into a cocktail glass. Serve.

'It was my Uncle George who discovered that alcohol was a food well in advance of modern medical thought.'

P. G. WODEHOUSE
The Inimitable Jeeves

Harry's Pick-Me-Up

This is a simple mixture that was served by Salvatore Calabrese during his tenure at London's Lanesborough Bar, but it could be made in any household – even by someone whose head is pounding and whose brain is stultified. The grenadine adds distinction to a standard pick-me-up.

30ml or 1 fl oz brandy
1 teaspoon grenadine
juice of half a lemon
Champagne

Shake all the ingredients, except the Champagne, in a cocktail shaker filled with ice. Strain into a Champagne flute, then top up with Champagne and serve.

Heart Starter

The rest of the world thinks of Australians as beer-drinkers. John Burgess of the Diamond Bar at the Menzies Hotel in Sydney, Australia, developed this recipe which, so they say, will dispatch the worst of a beer-induced hangover. A refinement of the treatment is to sniff the drink first so that the Pernod can be inhaled to clear the head and improve the feel and taste of the mouth.

about 23ml or ¾ fl oz Fernet Branca
about 23ml or ¾ fl oz crème de menthe
Pernod

Stir the first two ingredients over ice until well-chilled, then strain into a glass. Float a liberal dash of Pernod on top.

'This was a hangover. The real thing. Thank God he was dressed, he wouldn't have the dressing to go through, the fumbling with buttons, the insoluble puzzle that would be the shoelaces.'

CHARLES JACKSON
The Lost Weekend

Morning Spray

This drink is often recommended by barmen for people who, for some medical reason, are no longer to enjoy their couple of glasses of claret or malt whisky. For those who are still drinking, and have drunk too much the night before, Oliff, the head barman at the Royal Sydney Yacht Squadron in Sydney, Australia prescribed Morning Spray as a pick-me-up. It is also prescribed by the barman at the Reform Club in Pall Mall, London.

glass of tonic water
drop Angostura Bitters

Drop the bitters into the tonic water and stir.

Moulin Rouge

This nog, created by Ernie Muscatello and Bobby Taylor at the Hotel Tropicano in Las Vegas, has the advantage that the sometimes-stomach-churning appearance of egg yolk doesn't revolt the severely hungover. The disadvantage is that it therefore lacks the fat from the egg yolk which acts to a small extent as a breakfast substitute and prevents a collapse of the blood sugar once its initial effect has worn off.

30ml or 1 fl oz Old Tom gin
30 ml or 1 fl oz apricot brandy
¼ egg white
dash of grenadine

Combine all the ingredients and shake vigorously. Serve in cocktail glass.

Old Chappie

Many years ago, a contest was held to choose the best hangover cure served by the many bartenders at the Carnival Bar, Trinidad, in the West Indies. The winner was Faizool Ali, who recommended making a syrup by combining two cups of sugar and half a cup of water in a saucepan. He suggested that the hungover drinker should stir the mixture until the sugar dissolved, allow it to simmer until the liquid became clear, and then allow it to cool before being stored in the refrigerator.

30ml or 1 fl oz lime juice
about 22ml or ¾ fl oz bar syrup
225ml or 8 fl oz beer
dash Angostura bitters

Pour the ingredients over crushed ice in a 12-oz glass. Stir and serve with a straw.

Pheasant Runner

Despite its exotic name, few hard-core drinkers would be likely to rush for the pick-me-up offered by the Pheasant Run in St Charles, Illinois. The thought of combining beer, tomato juice and vodka is certainly not immediately attractive, but for those who feel so awful that there is no hope, the idea that anything could be better than nothing might prevail.

   30ml or 1 fl oz vodka
   90ml or 3 fl oz tomato juice
   175ml or 6 fl oz beer

Mix together and serve.

Port Flip

Here is a recipe that isn't a hangover cure, but is served as the night progresses when someone needs fortification so that they can keep going until the early hours. It is energy-providing, rather than curative. Barman Dale DeGroff recommends it, but it comes with a warning. It contains quite a kick, so that if you are one of those drinkers who keeps a check on what they are taking and the night is still not over, don't forget to include this in the score.

60ml or 2 fl oz ruby port
30ml or 1 fl oz brandy
1 free-range egg yolk
freshly grated nutmeg

Pour all the ingredients into a cocktail shaker filled with ice. Shake. Strain into a small wine glass. Garnish with a dusting of freshly grated nutmeg.

Prairie Oyster

The Prairie Oyster is a regular remedy that will be offered by most barmen. It tastes as unpleasant as one of the stories about the origin of its name. 'Prairie oysters' in the cattle-raising areas of the United States was the local term for calves' testicles, after the cattle had been castrated and their redundant organs had been fried for breakfast.

This is the memorable story that goes with the name of the drink, but whether the breakfast dish was named after the drink or the drink after the dish is uncertain. There is no doubt that the egg floating in the glass does look like a disembodied eyeball. Not one for the squeamish!

There are many variations on the Prairie Oyster. At its most basic, it is non-alcoholic, but this particular recipe includes port, for its hair of the dog status. In France, port is widely used to settle upset stomachs, so its inclusion in this drink may just allow you to keep the lot down.

virgin olive oil
1 tablespoon tomato ketchup
1 free-range egg yolk
dash Worcestershire sauce
dash white-wine vinegar
dash freshly ground black pepper
45ml or 1½ fl oz port

Rinse the wine glass with the olive oil and discard the oil. Add the tomato ketchup and egg yolk (don't break the yolk) and season with Worcestershire sauce, vinegar, and add pepper to taste. Pour in the port and drink it down → quickly.

Red Snapper

A variation on a Bloody Mary. Made with gin, not vodka, it's said to have been a favourite of John Jacob Astor, served by Parisian barman Fernand Petiot who worked at the King Cole Bar in New York's St Regis Hotel.

150ml or 5 fl oz tomato juice
dash of fresh lemon juice
30ml or 1 fl oz gin
pinch of celery salt
2 dashes Worcestershire sauce
2 dashes Tabasco sauce
freshly ground black pepper

Fill a highball glass with ice-cubes, then pour in the tomato and lemon juices. Add the gin, celery salt and sauces and stir. Add a quick twist of black pepper. Garnish with a wedge of lime on the rim, and a stalk of celery, if requested. Serve with a stirrer.

'I was left in no doubt about the severity of the hangover when a cat stamped into the room.'

P. G. WODEHOUSE

'When you wake up alone after consuming a whole dictionary of cocktails, your body is on red alert. Keep perfectly still. Imagine that you have a crate of unstable nitroglycerine lodged in your brain and that with one false move you'll be painted over the bedroom walls.'

KEITH FLOYD
Floyd on Hangovers

Ritz Reviver

A standard restorative for those whose excesses the night before have left them within striking distance of the Paris Ritz. If you want to keep going throughout the day and your hangover is moderate to severe, it would be as well to have some breakfast, too, so that you don't relapse after the effect of the Ritz Reviver wears off.

  twist of orange peel
  30ml or 1 fl oz Fernet Branca
  30ml or 1 fl oz crème de menthe
  dash Angostura bitters

Rub the rim of a cocktail glass with the orange peel. Shake the remaining ingredients in a cocktail shaker filled with ice. Strain into a cocktail glass. Drop in the twist of orange peel, and serve.

Rosa's Magical Cure

This is the concoction used by Salvatore Calabrese, created by his mother when she saw he needed revitalizing, and it was his first encounter with a hangover cure. He remembers the sensation of many layers of flavours, ranging from the sweetness of Marsala and the sharpness of lemon juice, to the spice of chilli and the egg that binds it together.

1 free-range egg yolk
pinch ground chilli pepper
1 small teaspoon fresh lemon juice
30ml or 1 fl oz sweet Marsala

Place the egg yolk, without breaking it, in a small glass. Add the chilli pepper and lemon juice, then the Marsala. Don't stir it. Drink it all down in one gulp. Serve with a fresh zabaglione to follow; this gives you even more energy.

Salvamento!

Another variation of the eggnog theme, but this one's interest lies in its place of origin. It was devised by Horacio Tamayo, a bartender at Sanborn's Bar, Mexico City, who found it so effective that he named it *Salvamento*, meaning 'life-saving'.

1 egg, beaten
juice of 1 lemon
1 teaspoon sugar
30ml or 1 fl oz gin
soda water

Pour all the ingredients, except the soda water, into a cocktail shaker filled with ice. Shake well. Strain into a highball glass filled with ice and top up with soda water.

Sangrita Cocktail

A traditional Mexican drink, and a good party tipple, or useful the following morning if you've overdone it. Make it at least a couple of hours before your guests arrive. Simply leave out the Tequila to make the non-alcoholic Sangrita.

Serves 10

300ml or 10 fl oz Tequila

1 litre or 35 fl oz tomato juice

450ml or 16 fl oz fresh orange juice

5 teaspoons clear honey

90ml or 3 fl oz fresh lime juice

1 chilli, finely chopped

2 teaspoons finely chopped white onion

pinch salt and freshly ground black pepper, to taste

10 drops Worcestershire sauce

Pour all ingredients into a mixing bowl; stir well. Chill for two hours, then strain into a large pitcher. Serve in wine glasses.

Sazerac

This is a hangover cure that tastes like the strongest old-fashioned medicine. It follows the rule that if the remedy doesn't taste both strong and slightly repellent, it is unlikely to do any good. On this principle alone, Sazerac should defeat the worst of hangovers in a flash

30ml or 1 fl oz Pernod
30ml or 1 fl oz whisky
1 dash Angostura bitters
1 teaspoon sugar

Pour all ingredients into a cocktail shaker filled with ice. Shake. Strain and serve with a lemon twist.

Suffering Bastard

The Suffering Bastard was introduced to the world by Shepheard's Hotel in Cairo. Shepheard's was one of the places made deservedly famous (or notorious) by the great writers of yesteryear such as Somerset Maugham or Ernest Hemingway. Here is where the great and the good, diplomats and conmen, soldiers and travellers, writers and journalists met, plotted, wined and dined.

Angostura bitters
15ml or ½ fl oz gin
15ml or ½ fl oz brandy
1 teaspoon lime juice
cold ginger ale

Swirl the bitters around a highball glass and toss the excess. Half-fill the glass with ice and add the gin, brandy, lime juice and ginger ale. Garnish with slices of lime, cucumber and orange. Add a sprig of mint on the rim.

Stomach Reviver

A herbal remedy incorporating the ubiquitous Fernet Branca. Its multitude of herbs are said to both quieten an upset stomach, and settle disturbed nerves. It is a short drink and can be drunk in one go. Later it would be as well to supplement its effects with a long glass of orange juice and, preferably, some breakfast.

30ml or 1 fl oz Fernet Branca
30ml or 1 fl oz brandy
3 dashes Angostura bitters

Pour all ingredients into a cocktail shaker filled with ice. Shake. Strain into a shot glass, then knock it back and breathe a sigh of relief.

Sympathy

A drink that feels your pain. It was devised by the barman at the Duke at the Half Moon Bar, Amsterdam, in Holland. *Brandewign*, the constituent that provides its alcoholic content, is a smooth Dutch liquor meaning 'burned wine'. The same term has been in use for hundreds of years, but over the course of time in England it became corrupted to 'brandy-wine' and later abbreviated to 'brandy'.

> *1 whole egg*
> *30ml or 1 fl oz lemon juice*
> *15-22ml or ½ - ¾ fl oz sugar syrup (to taste)*
> *45ml or 1½ fl oz Brandewign (or vodka)*
> *Soda to taste*

Pour all ingredients, except the soda, into a cocktail shaker and shake vigorously. Strain into a glass filled with ice. Top up with soda.

Thomas Abercrombie

This is a classic hangover remedy that combines both an antacid with a hair of the dog. Its single failing is the call for golden Tequila, which is going to contain more congeners than the clear type. It is named, by the way, after the man whose research uncovered the formula.

> *2 Alka Selzer tablets*
> *1 double shot of José Cuervo Tequila Gold*

Drop the tablets into the liquor and allow to fizz for four seconds before drinking.

Tokyo Bloody Mary

Another variation on the ever-popular Bloody Mary. Because the Japanese and other Far Eastern people have a different enzyme system for metabolizing alcohol, this form of Bloody Mary is made with rice wine as its main alcoholic ingredient, which has a lower ABV than vodka.

30ml or 1 fl oz saké
125ml or 4 fl oz tomato juice
20ml or about ⅔ fl oz fresh lemon juice
8 dashes Tabasco sauce
4 dashes Worcestershire sauce
4 dashes medium sherry
pinch of celery salt
pinch of black pepper

Pour all the ingredients into cocktail shaker filled with ice. Shake. Strain into a highball glass filled with ice. Garnish with a stick of celery. Serve.

'Let us have wine and women,
mirth and laughter,
Sermons and soda-water
the day after.'

Geoge Gordon, Lord Byron

Vampire

A popular drink in Mexico — so popular, in fact, that it is frequently described as Mexico's national drink. It combines a variety of flavours, of orange, tomato juice, spices, honey and onion. It doesn't sound promising, but if it is made and left to settle overnight, it is surprisingly drinkable, especially if served well-chilled. As it can be made in advance, the number of ingredients is not a deterrent to making it.

The variety of spices in the drink is capable of bringing to life even the most jaded taste bud. The drink is rich in vitamins, as it contains tomatoes, orange juice, lime and chilli. The honey and onion provide calories, some in the form of a rapidly absorbed sugar, the rest as a complex carbohydrate so that there will be a lasting benefit.

75ml or about 2½ fl oz tomato juice
30ml or 1 fl oz fresh orange juice
30ml or 1 fl oz silver Tequila
1 teaspoon clear honey
10ml or about ⅓ fl oz fresh lime juice
half a slice of onion, finely chopped
a few slices fresh red-hot chilli
a few drops Worcestershire sauce
salt, to taste

Pour all the ingredients into a cocktail shaker filled with ice. Shake well to release the flavour of the chilli. Strain into a highball glass filled with ice. Garnish with a wedge of lime on the rim.

Wake-Up Call

Salvatore Calabrese created this for New Year's Day after the millennium, when the prevalence of sore heads reached record numbers. Hair of the dog is well-represented, so it will need to be followed by the obligatory long glass of cool fruit juice and some cereals.

> *30ml or 1 fl oz vodka*
> *20ml or about ⅔ fl oz Cointreau*
> *10ml or about ⅓ fl oz fresh lemon juice*
> *90ml or 3 fl oz tomato juice*
> *Tabasco sauce*
> *pinch celery salt*
> *pinch caster sugar*
> *Champagne*

Pour all the ingredients, except the Champagne, into a cocktail shaker filled with ice. Shake. Pour into a highball glass filled about three-quarters with ice. Top up with Champagne. Stir. Garnish with a wedge of lime.

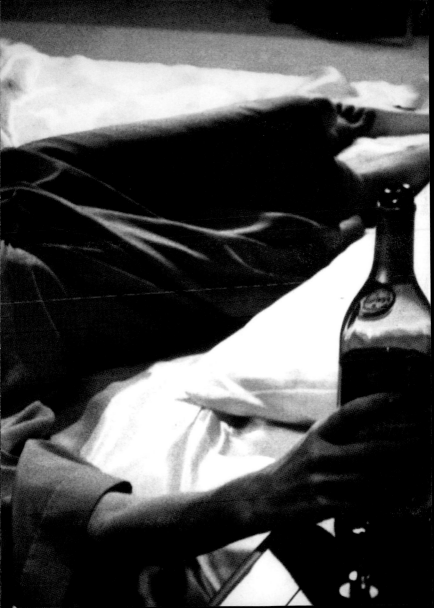

White Swan

An attractive name for a drink based on sherry, honey and egg yolk. It follows the scientific principle of combining sugars, a taste of alcohol and the fat and protein of egg yolk. It was invented by Joe Familoe of the Three Swans Pub at Forest Hills Inn, Long Island, New York. The drink is a short, down-in-one-shot type. To deal with the dehydration, orange juice to follow is probably best.

45ml or 1½ fl oz sherry
1 teaspoon honey
1 egg yolk
milk
freshly grated nutmeg

Mix the first three ingredients well and add them to a tumbler of cold milk. Sprinkle with fresh nutmeg.

'An intelligent man is sometimes forced to be drunk to spend time with fools.'

ERNEST HEMINGWAY

Drinks, Juices & Smoothies

Not everyone who's is hungover wants more of the hair of the dog that bit them. The following section thus offers recipes for hangover cures that contain no alcohol, but are based, for the most part, on fresh fruit juices. When choosing fruit, try to buy it as fresh as possible, and make sure it is as chemical-free as possibly; choose organic if you can. Ideally fruit should be picked straight from the garden or hedgerow, (provided it isn't too close to passing traffic), and eaten immediately.

Allegria

There is no hair of the dog in this one — just a cool, refreshing drink. It isn't calorie-rich, so once you're feeling better you will have to boost your blood sugar with other foods, but it does provide some much-needed fluid while you wait for nature to take its course.

half a ripe mango, peeled, cut and diced
60ml or 2 fl oz carrot juice
60ml or 2 fl oz pineapple juice
60ml or 2 fl oz fresh orange juice
20ml or about ⅔ oz fresh lemon juice
still mineral water

Put the mango in a blender. Add all other ingredients (except the water), a scoop of ice-cubes, and blend. Pour into a goblet full of fresh ice. Fill to three-quarters full. Dilute with water to taste and stir. Garnish with a slice of orange and a maraschino cherry. Serve with a straw.

Blood-Sugar Tonic

Juices and smoothies are natural pick-me-ups, containing all the minerals, vitamins and antioxidants found in the fruit and vegetables that go into them. This tonic, made from alfalfa sprouts, was also created by Salvatore Calabrese, who found that his customers welcome the kick it gives and the aniseed flavour of the fennel.

225g or 8oz alfalfa sprouts
225g or 8oz mung bean sprouts
225g or 8oz lentil sprouts
2 kale leaves
225g or 8oz Jerusalem artichokes
1 handful string beans
1 medium parsnip
115g or 4oz cup fennel

Wash all vegetables and push through a juicer or blender. Serve over ice.

Blueberry Breezer

Blueberries rival cranberries as the berries of choice to restore vitamin levels and provide essential trace elements. In addition, they're loaded with antioxidants that preserve the arteries and keep cancers at bay. The best are the wild ones, but all varieties are excellent to eat – and they're becoming much more readily available. Blueberries are good for health and, when juiced, turn the most mundane drink into a delight.

> *3 passion fruit*
> *1 mango, peeled and stoned*
> *125g or 4oz blueberries*
> *ice*
> *mineral water*

Take the flesh of the passion fruit. Mix it with the mango, then with the blueberries and place all the ingredients in a blender. The amount of mineral water will depend on the consistency you prefer.

Carrot Comfort

In the decadent Swinging Sixties, pretty women met their dissolute friends in the juice bar at Harrods in London to have a reviving drink of carrot juice. The memory of childhood during the Second World War, when carrots were obligatory eating, encouraged the ravers. Ginger added to carrot juice settles the stomach and fortifies the spirits. Although ginger has been a popular ingredient of medicines for generations, it has also been used by tired lovers as an aphrodisiac.

200g or 7oz carrots
1 apple
1cm or ½ inch fresh root ginger
ice

Clean, top and tail the carrots and scrub them. Wash the apple. Cut them and the ginger into small pieces and blend. Serve in chilled glasses over ice.

Cherry Delight

This is a drink that makes full use of the traditional fruits of the British or American garden. Cherries give it an unusual taste, and are thought to act as a restorative because of their high vitamin content. The mixture of apples, pears and cherries is also rich in flavonoids and potassium as well as vitamin C. Apples and pears are good sources of pectin, a valuable soluble fibre.

1 apple, chopped, peeled and quartered
1 pear, skinned and chopped
375g or 13oz cherries

Place all ingredients into a blender and blend until smooth. This drink can be diluted to taste with ice and sparkling mineral water.

Cranberry Crush

A long, refreshing drink, which has cranberry juice as its base. Cranberry juice is one of the most nutritious of all juices. Although famous for keeping urinary infections at bay, it is also cleansing to the gums and mouth. It is rich in vitamin C, potassium, folic acid and has the unusual powers of preventing bacteria from sticking to the inside of the mouth, gums and bladder.

1 orange
55g or 2oz apples
100ml or 3½ fl oz cranberry juice
ice

Peel the orange and extract the juice of it and the peeled apple. Mix in the cranberry juice and serve with ice in a long glass.

Grapefruit Refresher

Fifty years ago, grapefruit was the fruit no smart breakfast table would be without. Now the profusion of other tropical fruits has driven it away, and its sharp taste is almost forgotten. To make this reviving drink, mix grapefruit with oranges and lemon. One word of warning, however: several drugs, when metabolized in the body, use the same enzyme as grapefruit juice. This may interfere with the action of the drug and can result in the drinker having a greater effective dose than he or she expects. Consult your doctor before using this recipe if you're on any type of medication.

> 2 grapefruit
> 2 oranges
> 1 lemon

Peel all three fruits, remove any pips and blend the fruits together. Pour the juice into a long glass, adding ice to taste.

'Alcohol is a good preservative for everything but brains.'

MARY PETTIBONE POOLE

Homemade Lemonade

People born before the days of antibiotics and central heating remember their childhood illnesses of measles and mumps because of the roaring fire that was lit in their bedrooms and the jugs of homemade lemonade beside their beds.

Homemade lemonade has escaped from the sickroom and is now a drink that can be served with any meal. It still has a role for treating the sick, including those who have fallen prey to the injudicious drinking of alcohol. There is nothing like homemade lemonade on returning home in the evening (and again the next morning) to relieve the dehydration and hypoglycaemia.

This recipe comes from Rose Elliot, the food writer. It becomes better the longer it stands in the refrigerator. Overnight is fine and it will still taste fresh for lunch the next day.

5 large unwaxed organic lemons
750ml or 25 fl oz water
100-200g or 3½-7oz granulated sugar
ice-cubes
sprigs of fresh mint

Scrub the lemons, then grate the rind from three of them, using a fine grater or zester. Be careful not to get any of the white pith; vitamin-rich as it is, it could give the lemonade a bitter taste. Put the zest into a large bowl or jug. Squeeze the juice from all the lemons and add to the jug, along with the water and the smaller quantity of sugar. Stir and chill. This becomes better the longer it stands; overnight is fine. Add some more sugar to taste, if necessary, then strain the lemonade into a serving jug filled with ice. Garnish with sprigs of fresh mint, if desired.

Honey Bun

Not everyone who feels lousy can attribute the feeling to alcohol. Teetotallers are not always at their best between 7am and 9am on a damp day. They, too, need energy-providing drinks. This one provides sugar, protein and traces of fat and minerals with the yogurt. The banana is rich in potassium and other nutrients. For those with a hangover, this energy-generating drink would soothe the stomach and restore the blood sugar.

half a ripe banana
1 teaspoon clear honey
2 teaspoons natural yogurt
water

Place all ingredients into a blender and blend until smooth. Add a little water in the blender if you prefer a longer drink. Pour into a highball glass filled with ice.

Iced Mint Tea

Iced tea is reminiscent of garden parties or tea on holiday in North Africa or the Middle East. It is refreshing, contains a rich supply of antioxidants and, if taken with sugar, provides a quick lift to blood-sugar levels. The tea also rehydrates a body drained by excesses of the previous night. It should be accompanied by buttered toast and, preferably, some form of protein, such as a boiled egg or a rasher or two of bacon.

125ml or 4 fl oz cold tea

3 sprigs fresh mint

ice

sugar to taste

Make the tea before you go out and put it in the refrigerator overnight. Pour it into a long glass, add fresh mint and sugar to taste. Slowly sip it while waiting for the world to return to normal so that you can nibble the toast without feeling too nauseated.

Indian Summer

Not everyone likes the bitter taste of cranberries. Most proprietary cranberry juices are already sold blended with other fruits that take away their tartness. This great combination features cranberry juice sweetened by a pear.

1 large pear, peeled and quartered
100ml or 3½ fl oz cranberry juice
ice-cubes

Juice the pear and mix it with the cranberry juice. Serve with ice.

Kiwi Punch

Kiwi fruit is amazingly rich in vitamin C. It also contains vitamin A, potassium and folic acid. A mixture of oranges and kiwi fruits with a dash of lemon provides a vitamin-packed punch to carry you through the day.

2 oranges
2 kiwi fruits
ice-cubes
dash of lemon juice

Peel the oranges and put them in the blender. The kiwi fruits don't need to be skinned (unless you prefer), as the peels are full of vitamins. Place the ice in a glass and pour on the fruit mixture.

Mellow Melon

This easy recipe makes a refreshing drink that appeals to the idle drinker, and it's perfect for breakfast. Melon has enough water in it for this to be a thirst-quencher, but it's also rich in vitamins A and C and potassium. A glass of this also contains an appreciable dose of folic acid.

500g or 1lb cantaloupe
ice-cubes

Peel the melon, remove the pips and blend. Pour over ice and drink.

Papaya Pick-Me-Up

Papayas are rich in vitamins, and this exotic drink will refresh memories of the Caribbean even as it tops up the blood with vitamins A and C. These fruits are also a good source of trace elements such as magnesium, potassium and selenium.

125g or 4oz papaya, peeled and deseeded
2 oranges, peeled
125g or 4oz cucumber, peeled
ice

Juice the peeled papaya, oranges and cucumber and serve over ice.

Papaya Shake

Another famous drink from Axel Gorlach of the Rama Hotel in Bangkok, Thailand, who also gave the world the Bullshot (*see* page 82). This drink makes use of a variety of fresh fruit juices that brighten the dreariest morning — especially if it's complicated by a sore head. Taken regularly, it would provide a good mixture of vitamins and minerals.

1 papaya
1 small ripe banana
1 glass milk
1 whole egg
1 teaspoon sugar

Peel the papaya and scoop out the seeds; discard. Chop the flesh roughly and place in the blender. Add a few ice-cubes. Add the rest of the ingredients and blend everything until smooth. Serve in large tumblers.

Passion Fruit Smoothie

This is a smoothie to have early in the morning with toast. It's easier to digest than a standard breakfast, but will serve to raise the blood sugar and to keep it at a reasonable level well into the morning. When dealing with all citrus fruits such as orange or grapefruit, as much pith as possible should be left on the segments, even if the pips are removed. It is the pith that is richest in vitamins, antioxidants and trace elements. Some people leave the pips of fruits such as the passion fruit in the mixture so that the organic chemicals within them may add to the vitamins and trace elements.

flesh of 2 passion fruits
1 mango, peeled and stone removed
150ml or 5 fl oz low-fat yogurt
300ml or 10 fl oz skimmed milk

Put all ingredients in a blender and blend until smooth. Drink through a straw.

Peach Perfection

Ginger was the basis for many of doctors' medicines in the nineteenth century. It eased the stomach, soothed the guts and alleviated pains in the joints. Mixed with peach, it is as appetizing as it is health-giving.

250g or 9oz peaches
fresh ginger, to taste
6 mint leaves
sparkling mineral water

Blend the juice of the peach with the ginger. Pour over ice and add enough water to top up the glass. Decorate with mint leaves.

Plum Perfect

This respected and natural hangover cure is made by mixing red grapes, blackberries and plums. The deep colour of the drink, which is popular in high summer, will cheer up the most jaded drinker even before the juice has been absorbed into the system.

100g or 3½ oz red grapes
100g or 3½ oz blackberries
100g or 3½ oz plums
ice-cubes
still mineral water

The fruit should be blended and poured onto ice-cubes in the waiting glass. Top up to the desired consistency with still mineral water.

Pussyfoot Cocktail

For those who don't like alcohol the morning after. The Pussyfoot Cocktail contains all the old favourite juices and is a classic hangover cure.

30ml or 1 fl oz fresh lime juice
30ml or 1 fl oz fresh lemon juice
30ml or 1 fl oz fresh orange juice
grenadine, to taste
maraschino cherry, for decoration

Mix all the ingredients together in a cocktail shaker already packed with ice and then strain into a glass. Add a cherry for a final flourish.

Strawberry Surprise

Strawberries are now available for most of the year. Mixed with pineapples and a banana to add some potassium, they are as refreshing as they are invigorating. This drink may be sipped slowly through a straw, or it can be diluted with ice. Either way, it will provide a hefty dose of vitamin C, magnesium and, thanks to the banana, potassium.

100g or 3½ oz strawberries
300g or 10½ oz pineapple, chopped and peeled
1 banana, peeled

Juice the strawberries and pineapple. Add the banana and some ice-cubes and blend. Drink slowly and enjoy.

Virgin Lea

An award-winning non-alcoholic cocktail that is a firm favourite of barmen worldwide when they are looking for a drink that is spicy, sharp and sweet.

125ml or 4 fl oz tomato juice
60ml or 2 fl oz passion fruit juice
¼ yellow bell pepper, sliced
1 teaspoon clear honey
2 dashes Worcestershire sauce
ice-cubes
cherry tomato and basil sprigs, for garnish

Place the pepper slices in a blender and add the juices. Blend for ten seconds at low speed. Add the honey, Worcestershire sauce and a few ice-cubes. Blend at high speed for ten seconds. Pour through a strainer into a highball glass filled with ice-cubes. Garnish with a cherry tomato speared with a basil sprig. Serve with a straw and a stirrer.

Virgin Mary

A non-alcoholic Bloody Mary. Its additional ingredients make it a spicy drink, even without an alcoholic component.

150ml or 5 fl oz tomato juice
30ml or 1 fl oz fresh lemon juice
2 dashes Worcestershire sauce
dash Tabasco sauce
salt and freshly ground black pepper
1 stick celery

Pour the first four ingredients into a highball glass filled with ice-cubes. Season to taste. Stir well. Add the celery stick to use as a stirrer.

'Use a little wine for thy stomach's sake
and thy frequent infirmities.'

ST PAUL,
Timothy 5:23

Drinking to Your Health

The secret of drinking healthily is to drink in moderation. Every drink by containing alcohol includes a substance that in small quantities is beneficial, but which in large amounts is poisonous. Some forms of drink, especially red wines grown in a warm, moist climate, have additional advantages over and above those provided by the alcohol. They contain antioxidants that are beneficial to the heart, blood vessels and to the constituents of the blood so that the blood clots less easily. Binge drinking is always dangerous, even if the drinker is accustomed to alcohol.

Maintaining a Quality of Life

The good news for drinkers sobering up with the help of hangover cures is that provided they don't make a habit of heavy drinking, a modest daily intake will actually help them to live longer. Not only will they enjoy a longer life more by having two or three glasses of wine, a pint and a half of beer or three tots of whisky daily, but they will have a better intellect with which to enjoy it. This is because an increasing amount of evidence indicates that, so long as someone doesn't drink to the point of inducing alcoholic dementia, they are less likely to develop Alzheimer's Disease. Drinkers have been shown to live through a happier and more social old age, with a greater chance of recognizing their friends and family.

Admittedly, Alzheimer's Disease is more common in heavy drinkers, but it is less common in those who drink in moderation. What is fascinating and should please those now enjoying the hair of the dog is that even those people who gave up drinking in early middle age will still be less likely to develop senile dementia later than those who have never drunk at all.

Drinking and the Heart

The apparently paradoxical effect of alcohol on the intellect — overdoing it causes an immediate loss of intelligence but a regular small amount is advantageous — is related to its beneficial effect on the cardiovascular system. If the blood supply to the brain is maintained, the drinker's memory will be preserved.

This benefit of alcohol has been accepted by many doctors for centuries, but the process by which it improves the action of the heart and the cardiovascular system has only become apparent over the last forty years. Until the first half of the twentieth century, when the pursuit of health through cultivating a healthy lifestyle with a good diet and plenty of exercise became firmly established, doubts were rarely cast on the health benefits of small quantities of alcohol.

It seemed perverse to suggest that a substance that is poisonous in excess could have so many advantages, yet for well over two thousand years, since the days of Hypocrites and Galen, doctors had recommended alcohol not only as a tonic but for its curative powers, and even as a means of preventing infection and many chronic diseases.

From the 1970s onwards, evidence accumulated that alcohol taken in moderation reduced the incidence of heart disease so that its effect on the cause of death of those who drank wisely made an impact on the national mortality statistics. Even so, in the second half of the twentieth century, many doctors were still not prepared to believe this evidence; fortunately, help was at hand from an unlikely source.

Sir Richard Doll, one of the greatest physicians of the twentieth century, agreed that people who had up to four drinks ('units') of alcohol a day were less likely to have a heart attack and were therefore likely to live longer. As Doll was the doctor who first proved the link between smoking and lung cancer, his opinion carried great weight. Today, few doctors don't agree that alcohol in general, and red wine in particular, protects the heart and arteries, provided that it is taken in modest amounts.

Of course, research into the benefits of alcohol was not confined to the United Kingdom. In addition to Dr Alan Bailey in London, Dr Selwyn St Ledger at the

Medical Research Council in Cardiff, and Professor Tom Whitehead in Birmingham, Dr Klatsky in the United States and Dr Serg Renaud in France also showed that there were benefits to the health of those politely described as 'light to moderate drinkers'.

In the United States, a survey begun in the early 1970s investigated the effects of drinking on nearly 90,000 female nurses. It has shown that the advantage to modest drinkers from a reduction in heart disease outweighs any of the known disadvantages of alcohol to health. Even more remarkably, *all* causes of death – not just death among those who benefit from a reduction in heart disease – is reduced. The facts are plain: social drinkers live longer, whether they are male or female.

The advantages of alcohol may be demonstrated by plotting death rate against alcohol consumption. It is found that those who drink more than six units a day die younger. The men who drink under three or four units a day and the women who drink fewer than two or three (one or two do even better) live longer. Teetotallers are apt to die at about the same rate as those who have six drinks daily.

While we know that small quantities of alcohol are beneficial to the cardiovascular system by protecting against furred-up arteries, and hence heart attacks and strokes, there is no simple explanation for this mechanism. Alcohol, whether in beer, wine or spirits, affects the nature of the cholesterol in the blood. The cholesterol that does the damage is the low-density lipoprotein (LDL) cholesterol. This oozes out of arterial walls and helps to form a potentially dangerous blob of fatty material, known as an atheromatous plaque, on the inside of arterial walls. The blob may break down; if it ruptures, its contents become the basis of a clot that blocks an artery. Once an artery in the heart is blocked, the heart muscle is starved of blood — and therefore oxygen and nutrients — and is destroyed. The person suffers a heart attack. Alcohol reduces the amount of dangerous LDL cholesterol and increases the proportion of high-density lipoprotein, or HDL, cholesterol. HDL cholesterol is not dangerous; in fact, it is actually life-saving.

Alcohol also affects the stickiness of the platelets: the small particles in the blood that form clots. If the platelets don't stick together, a clot is less likely to form if any atheroma (fatty debris) escapes into the bloodstream. Not only are the fatty blobs, the plaques, less likely to rupture, but clots are not so liable to form around them in those who drink in reasonable quantities. Furthermore, alcohol in moderation improves the state of the fibres in the arterial wall.

The story doesn't end here. Wine drinkers, especially red-wine drinkers, have an advantage over those who drink other drinks, even if they all drink in moderation only. Red wine contains antioxidants. Oxidizing free radicals in the blood damage the blood vessels and therefore hasten the formation of the fatty blobs within the arteries. Fortunately, these free radicals can be neutralized by antioxidants. Red wine made from grapes grown in warm, moist climates is one of the best sources of antioxidants which, when taken in modest amounts, keep the lining of the arteries glistening and clean.

However, nobody nursing a hangover should think that the advantages of alcohol for light to modest drinkers is extended to heavy drinkers. Half of all the middle-aged and older men who die suddenly are heavy drinkers. Not all of this, however, is directly related to alcohol. Many such men are also heavy smokers, are overweight and take too little exercise. Yet heavy drinking – especially if it's binge drinking – undoubtedly has a bad effect on blood pressure and metabolism, and hence on the arteries.

Binge drinking also increases the blood pressure and this may induce rupture of one of these fatty blobs (atheromatous plaques) in a coronary artery. Even in younger binge drinkers, sudden death is not uncommon. If a careful record is kept of all those admitted to casualty who have had a heart attack or a stroke, it is found that the number of patients with these troubles increases on Friday and Saturday nights. Why Friday and Saturday nights? Because these are the classic binge-drinking nights.

There is one strange statistic about these binge-drinking deaths among those who are not usually heavy drinkers. The death rate is increased regardless of the type of drink, unless they have been having red wine. There is no appreciable increase in strokes and heart attacks among the red-wine drinkers.

The adverse effects of heavy drinking are not confined to its influence on sudden death from high blood pressure, heart attacks and strokes. Persistently heavy drinkers may develop a relatively rare condition known as a cardiac myopathy. Everyone knows that, as he or she grows older, the persistent drinker develops spindly, feeble limbs and a fat tummy and chest. Yet it is not only the legs and arms that become weak; the heart muscle is also altered, and as the muscle power within the heart alters, the heart itself becomes enlarged and feeble. This damage to the heart muscle, known as myopathy, results in a form of heart failure that is notoriously difficult to treat.

Heavy, persistent drinkers may therefore not only suffer sudden death, they may also die a slow one from a type of heart failure that is almost impossible to treat.

Drinking and High Blood Pressure

There is an obvious link between high blood pressure, arterial disease, heart attacks and strokes. The effect of alcohol on blood pressure is complex. In most people, blood pressure goes down immediately after drinking because their blood vessels are dilated and they are relaxed. However, there is a rebound effect as, later, the blood pressure rises to a level higher than that which existed before they started to drink.

A rise in blood pressure may precipitate a heart attack or a stroke. Persistent drinkers eventually develop a persistently raised blood pressure. The good news is that often this will return to normal if the patient adopts a more reasonable drinking pattern.

It has been suggested that the persistently raised blood pressure found in heavy drinkers is due to the fact that they tend to put on weight. Careful analysis of the figures has shown that although this is a factor, alcohol has a specific effect on blood pressure, independent of any increase in weight of the person. Thus, alcohol is a more important influence on blood pressure than weight.

The older the drinker, the more likely the alcohol is to affect his or her blood pressure. Whatever the drinker's age, it cannot be too strongly stressed that, despite the firmly held belief by many people that raised blood pressure is the result of mixing the grape and the grain (wine and beer, or beer and spirit), this is nonsense.

The increase in blood pressure after someone has been drinking, and the persistent rise if they continue drinking, is a direct effect of alcohol. It doesn't matter if they stick to beer all evening, or only drink whisky and water (which is less fattening), or only have wine because it is better for the coronary arteries; their blood pressure is still likely to rise if they drink too much alcohol.

Drinking and the Liver

Ninety per cent of the alcohol that is drunk is detoxified by the liver. Alcohol dehydrogenase, the enzyme that processes alcohol and enables it to be metabolized, is responsible for most of the detoxifying process, although there are other microsomal enzymes that play a part. (A microsome is a small cellular particle.) One of the differences between men and women when they drink is that the microsomal system is more efficient in men than in women. Similarly, after drinking, in men the dehydrogenase system begins to work at an earlier stage.

Over the past few years the amount of liver disease associated with heavy drinking in the UK has increased alarmingly. Even so, the majority of heavy drinkers will never develop the most severe forms of lasting liver problems. Eight or nine drinks a day or even only four pints of standard beer taken by a man who has the wrong genetic background could be enough to make him a candidate for cirrhosis if he keeps up this intake for years.

It is thus not only the quantity of alcohol that is drunk, but also the number of years this has continued.

Alcohol can be a cumulative poison. Fortunately, of all the heavy drinkers who take in as much as this, only one in five (some surveys have suggested as few as one in seven) will develop cirrhosis.

Women, however, are able to tolerate smaller quantities of alcohol than men. Should they drink as much as four or five drinks a day, they, too, could be in line for liver problems. A drink in this respect is ten grams of alcohol, and it makes no difference whether the alcohol is contained in a glass of gin or the most treasured claret. Ten grams of alcohol is equivalent to the present 'unit' in the UK (the measure varies from country to country). There is a hazard in trying to calculate how much alcohol someone has had as the strength of wine and beer varies, and the size of the glass has tended to increase over recent years. The old pub measure of a wine glass was a very small one, and these are now rarely used. The standard wine glass in the EU is 175ml, whereas before the UK joined, its standard wine glass was 125ml.

A unit is equivalent to half a pint (284ml) of ordinary strength lager, beer or cider which is typically 3.5 percent alcohol by volume (ABV). The standard

125ml wine glass when filled with a wine of twelve percent ABV is 1.5 units, and the 175ml glass of wine that makes up the new EU measure is equal to 2.1 units. Most wine these days is between eleven and fourteen percent ABV, appreciably stronger than twenty years ago. It is now unusual to find wines of low ABV, but these were comparatively common just twenty years ago.

In terms of spirits, a 25ml measure equals one unit, but spirits are now more usually served in a larger measure of 35ml. These changes and the differences between various types of beer and wine are important as they can lead to many people drinking more than they supposed.

The standard measure of sherry, port, Madeira and vermouth remains one unit. Alcopops, drinks that have only become popular over the last ten years, have confused the picture. A glass, just smaller than a half-pint mug, of 275ml of alcopop, which is usually five percent ABV (equivalent to one of the stronger beers) is 1.4 units.

The other factor that determines the likelihood of suffering permanent liver damage is the hereditary background of the drinker. There are some as yet unidentified inherited genes that seem to improve someone's ability to metabolize alcohol. It may be that people don't so much inherit a liver that is able to metabolize alcohol quickly, and therefore save them from a splitting headache and a terrible hangover the next day, but they may inherit a liver that enables them to continue drinking day after day without suffering damage.

On the other hand, there are probably people who are able to metabolize alcohol quickly, and thereby avoid a hangover, but may not be able to drink large quantities continuously. If such a person drinks alcohol, the liver deals with it immediately but the cumulative effect of a regular toxic daily dose is such that the liver first becomes infiltrated with fat and later becomes damaged irretrievably by scarring. This is known as cirrhosis. Most men, if they have the strength of mind to stop drinking when their liver is no more than overladen with fat, will make a full recovery and the liver won't progress to the cirrhotic stage. The tragedy is that this ability is not found in women.

Heavy-drinking women are likely to suffer cirrhosis if their liver ever becomes infiltrated with fat. Women are thus more vulnerable to long-term effects of alcohol.

Whatever the sex of the drinker, the good news is that before someone develops that first fatty infiltration, and later cirrhotic changes, they will have had to be drinking large quantities day after day for at least fifteen years.

A word of warning. It is unfair to assume that all cases of cirrhosis are the result of heavy drinking. There are other causes of cirrhosis of the liver and it needs an expert equipped with a powerful microscope and a piece of a person's liver to distinguish a case of cirrhosis caused by alcohol from one that has another cause. This, for example, could be hepatitis B, C or chronic heart failure. A little known but rather alarming fact is that gross obesity may be enough to induce cirrhosis, even if no alcohol is taken and there has never been exposure to hepatitis B or C.

It shouldn't be forgotten that fatty infiltration of the liver and cirrhosis are not the only troubles that can affect the liver of a heavy drinker. Acute alcoholic hepatitis is not only a very real danger, but a very sinister one. Some patients who develop acute alcoholic hepatitis suffer immediate liver failure as a result. Although the diagnosis of cirrhosis is one that is only confirmed by complex laboratory tests, it is possible by looking at one's fellow drinkers around the bar to spot those who have early signs of liver failure. Look at the palms of a heavy drinker. If the fleshy mounds of muscle at the base of their thumb and their little finger are unusually red, there is every chance that their level of circulating oestrogen is higher than usual.

Don't leap to conclusions. In women, these red palms may be because she is pregnant or because she is taking HRT or the pill. However in men there is no common reason for having high oestrogen levels, other than that their livers have been affected by alcohol and they are no longer detoxifying oestrogen as efficiently as they should.

High oestrogen levels that give someone 'liver palms' (bright-red palms) are also likely to give rise to dilated spider veins on the face and cheek. Nothing can be more distinctive than a ruddy complexion; it may even be associated with good health. But if it is because the little veins have been dilated by excessive alcohol, a drinker may be in trouble.

Although it is unlikely that this will be evident in a fellow drinker at the bar, he or she may also have these spider veins on their abdomens and chests. A few are accepted without suspicion, but too many spider veins on the tummy or chest and doubt is cast on the health of the liver.

To endorse the suspicion of heavy drinking, ask the man or post-menopausal woman in question to hold their hands outstretched, and look at them from the side. If there is a clearly delineated difference in colour between the back of the hand and the palm, and a line separates the two just as the Plimsoll line on the hull of a ship separates its two colours, then there is every likelihood that the person is a heavy drinker. A word of warning, however: there are other causes of high levels of oestrogen.

Although high levels of oestrogens can occur in both men as well as women drinkers, women who drink not only reasonably, but rather more than some people might think desirable, are likely to live longer than teetotallers. Even so, there can be disadvantages, and for this reason it is suggested that although most women can drink up to two or three units of alcohol a day without significant risks to their health, this shouldn't be exceeded. Heavy-drinking females are more likely to suffer from osteoporosis or from cancer of the breast. Conversely, they are less likely to suffer from heart disease post-menopausally, and drinking smaller amounts daily makes osteoporosis less likely.

Men who drink to the point at which their oestrogen levels are unusually high will not only develop liver palms and spider naevi on their face and chest, but they will display other physical signs of feminization. Their breasts will grow larger, their limbs more spindly and their chests and abdomen more plump. Meanwhile, their genitalia will shrink and they will lose their Tarzan-like chest hair.

Sex and Drinking

Alcohol doesn't only play havoc with the genital anatomy but also with its physiological function. Alcohol is a common cause of impotence; as Shakespeare reminded us, it increases the desire but decreases the ability. The 'brewer's droop' has become a commonly used term to describe the impotence that follows heavy drinking. In the most extreme cases, the man may not only suffer a brewer's droop but he may also nod off to sleep.

It shouldn't be thought that this problem only affects men. Women may find their desire heightened as their inhibitions disappear as quickly as the drink in their glasses, yet their lust is likely to be unsatisfied. In the same way that alcohol affects a man's erectile function, too much of it makes it difficult for a woman to have sex comfortably and, if she does, an orgasm is less likely. On the other hand, a man's ability the following morning after a disturbed, dream-ridden night may surprise him.

Kingsley Amis observed the following:

> 'Upon awakening: If your wife or other partner is beside you and, (of course), is

willing, perform the sexual act as vigorously as you can. The exercise will do you good, and — on the assumption that you enjoy sex — you will feel toned up emotionally.

'Warnings: (1) if you are in bed with somebody you should not be in bed with, and have IN THE LEAST DEGREE a bad conscience about this, abstain. Guilt and shame are prominent constituents of the metaphysical hangover, and will certainly be sharpened by indulgence on such an occasion.

'(2) For the same generic reason, do not take the matter into your own hands if you are awake and by yourself.'

The importance of an ability by a heavy drinker to have sex is as nothing compared to its possible effect on a woman, should she conceive. Alcohol may reduce fertility, just as cigarettes and cannabis do; however, it doesn't remove the potential to conceive. The standard teaching used to be that only very heavy-drinking females were in danger of having babies adversely affected by alcohol. Women who drank so much that they were obviously alcoholics may give birth to children with a classic physical and mental pattern of deformities: the so-called foetal alcohol syndrome. Children with foetal alcohol syndrome have pixie-like, low-slung ears; they have a greater space than usual between their nose and upper lip; a receding chin and an upturned nose. The little valley that most people have in their upper lips may be ironed out so that their long upper lip is stretched tight. Their eyes are smaller than usual and the difference in the skin folds around the eyes makes it appear as if they have a squint. Unfortunately, they may also have other, even more serious congenital abnormalities, including those affecting the heart and joints.

There is considerable evidence that, as in many conditions, the combination of smoking and alcohol is particularly damaging. A woman who both drinks, even if only socially, and smokes is liable to have a baby that is of appreciably lower birth rate than that of a child born to a woman who did neither.

Drinking in Pregnancy

Foetal alcohol syndrome is not found in the children of heavy social drinkers, so that it used to be supposed that social drinking in pregnancy was harmless. American research has shown that even social drinking may have an effect on an unborn child. This is known as the foetal alcohol affect. The child is likely to be smaller, to thrive less well after birth and to be less intelligent than would otherwise have been supposed. One unusual feature of the foetal alcohol effect is that children with it integrate less well with their contemporaries. It is always difficult to separate the effects of hereditary, congenitally acquired conditions and those that are related to a probably less than ideal environment after delivery.

The advice in the United States is that women should not drink at all when pregnant, and preferably not if there is any danger that they might become pregnant. British advice has been traditionally more liberal and pregnant women have been advised that they shouldn't drink more than two drinks (standard units) on any one occasion, and not more than three in a week.

Recently there has been a move among British doctors to veer towards the American point of view. One of the difficulties of adopting this hard line is that many women are unaware that they have conceived, and indeed, many women may conceive *because* they are drunk. Fortunately, the good news for them is that various surveys have failed to show any correlation between being drunk at the time of conception and abnormalities in the foetus — provided that the woman is usually a modest drinker and doesn't smoke.

The association between alcohol and bearing abnormal children was recognized in ancient Biblical times. When Samson's mother was pregnant, the prophet told her that she would bear a son and ordered her to stop drinking thusly: 'Thou shalt conceive and bear a son. Now drink no wine or strong drink.'

Drinking and Digestion

Many a household wakes to the sound of someone retching in the bathroom. All medical students learn that there are three principal causes of morning sickness. The person may be pregnant, they may be over-anxious or they may drink too much. Alcohol causes chronic gastritis, the stomach becomes permanently inflamed. In the same way the guts also become inflamed after regular over-indulgence. Alcohol is a common cause, but still only a minor cause, of irritable bowel syndrome, with all its distressing symptoms.

Sufferers from irritable bowel syndrome have noticed that the type of drink affects their symptoms. Just as those who suffer from a hangover are more likely to have one if the drink is dark and full of congeners, so may a patient with an irritable bowel be more likely to have its socially inconvenient symptoms. Quite apart from the effect of alcohol on people with irritable bowel syndrome, alcohol may have an effect on gut motility (motion) if someone is a regular heavy drinker.

Drinking and Weight

It is said that the dire effects of obesity will be the next great scourge to hit the developed world. This is attributed to too much reliance on calorie-dense convenience foods and too little exercise. Many doctors and nutritionalists fail to ask how much someone is drinking. When measuring calorie intake, it is not just alcoholic drinks that should be counted, but also soft drinks. This includes the mixers that dilute the gin or rum. Mixers may not only provide many of the calories, but they may also provide enough sugar to make gallstones more likely. Strangely, those who drink spirits but don't have calorie-rich mixers added to them are less likely to have gallstones than teetotallers. Add a mixer and gallstones are more commonly found.

It is not unusual for people to imbibe between 1,000 to 2,000 calories in fluid form daily. For many non-manual workers, this would be their total requirement for the day. The old reckoning that a glass of wine was about a hundred calories is now no longer true – at least in Europe Now that the standard wine glass has been increased to 175ml, it is at least 150 calories, and the fashionable dinner-party glass contains far more wine than this would represent. Half a pint of standard British beer was always assumed to contain 100 calories, yet the strength of beer in the UK has been creeping up, and with it, the calorie count. A tot of whisky is also larger than it was before the European Union was established and now provides about 100 calories. The tonic or bitter lemon that goes with it would be as much again.

It is well-known that the calorie content of Coca-Cola is high. In one recent study in Australia, it was found that a surprising number of people were having half their calorie intake in liquid form, mainly as non-alcoholic drinks. Most soft drinks are sweetened, and it doesn't matter if the sweetener is glucose or fructose (fruit sugars), or a mixture of both.

Every effort is made to encourage people to eat in bars. This delays the absorption of the alcohol and makes drunkenness and its consequences including the hangover less likely. However, most of the bar snacks, — the crisps, nuts and biscuits — are calorie-dense.

Drinking and the Nervous System

There is good and bad news about the effect of alcohol on the brain. As with most studies of alcohol and health, the good news is for those who drink in moderation, and the bad news is for the heavy drinkers.

As mentioned earlier, drinking in youth, even if it is given up in later life, tends to protect people from Alzheimer's Disease in old age. This discovery has never been completely explained. It has, however, been confirmed by different, reputable so-called 'twin studies'. In these studies the incidence of Alzheimer's Disease in a pair of twins is compared to their drinking habits at different times of their lives. These showed that drinking in moderation tended to reduce the likelihood of Alzheimer's.

The surprise of these research studies was that some of this protection was even enjoyed by those who drank when young, but became teetotal in middle age or older. The usual explanation of the benefits of alcohol in reducing the likelihood is that the brain's blood supply is improved. Alcohol in moderation is known to reduce

the amount of furring up that occurs in the carotid arteries. These are the arteries that lead from the great vessels in the chest through the neck and into the brain. If there is too much deposition of fatty atheroma in the carotids, the brain, which is already shrinking with age, may be deprived of necessary nutrients and oxygen and suffer additional damage.

Quite apart from the effect of a long-term modest alcohol intake on dementia, there is another unexpected finding. Contrary to popular belief, one small drink – a unit of alcohol – improves someone's intelligence quotient, otherwise known as the IQ. One standard drink raises the blood alcohol level by 15mg per 100ml, two standard drinks raises it to 30mg per 100ml. After the blood alcohol level has passed 30mg, the intelligence plummets, but surprisingly it is *increased* when it is around 15mg per 100ml.

This is sometimes said to be because the drinker is more confident and not beset by doubts when doing the intelligence test, but another equally possible explanation is that the blood supply to the brain has been improved and performance enhanced.

Alcohol Poisoning

Heavy drinking can produce acute alcohol poisoning. The brain cells suffer, but the good news is that they tend to be knocked out rather than killed. If they have an opportunity to recover, the intellect and the memory return once the cells pick up. Of course, prolonged heavy drinking produces different problems. If the heavy drinking is suddenly stopped, the person may suffer from a fit, a comparatively common cause of an otherwise inexplicable seizure.

In other cases they may suffer from delirium tremens, otherwise known as 'the DTs'. A person suffering from the DTs experiences a coarse tremor (shake) of the arms and legs, accompanied by daytime hallucinations, insomnia, horrendous nightmares and night sweats. The DTs are notorious not just because of these signs and symptoms but because of the hallucinations that sometimes accompany them. The person may feel that he is covered in crawling ants, or that rats and mice are all over him. The hallucinations may be visual, auditory (the rats may be squeaking) or sensory (sufferers may feel the rats crawling over their skin). The remarkable feature of the DTs is that an attack of it is associated with the cessation of drinking, rather than maintaining the existing high level. It is likely to be a withdrawal symptom when a previously heavy drinker suddenly stops. The treatment for the drinker is to be prescribed a tranquillizer for a short time after he has renounced the bottle.

The alteration in the metabolism caused by drinking and the effects it has on the absorption of vitamins from the guts may also damage the brain. One syndrome caused by vitamin deficiencies, Korsakoff's Syndrome, is a feature of prolonged heavy drinking. The drinker loses his memory, makes up stories to compensate for what he can't remember and shows other signs of dementia. Heavy drinkers may also develop a peripheral neuropathy, so that they lose the sensation in their feet, hands and lower limbs. These drinkers develop a characteristic walk. They have to stamp their feet, rather like a hackney pony, as otherwise they can't feel the ground beneath them.

When All Else Fails…

If the hangovers keep coming, whatever you do, there's always a last resort – Alcoholics Anonymous, or AA. It's drastic but it works. As the AA saying goes, 'If you don't take the first drink, you can't get drunk.' Nor can you get the hangover.

AA is for those who can't moderate their drinking and need to give up alcohol altogether. This self-help group is a collection of anonymous ex-drinkers who get together to help each other stay off the booze. It's an unusual charity that refuses to take money from outsiders, hires rooms rather than building expensive accommodation, and pays for itself by taking a collection at the meetings. There are all sorts of people at an AA group: men, women, young, old, rich and poor. AA drinking stories vary from the truly tragic to the howlingly funny, and a good AA meeting usually includes at least some laughter. Most countries now have AA groups and you can find your nearest in the UK by ringing the helpline 0845 769 7555 or visiting www.alcoholics-anonymous.org.uk. If you join AA, you need never have a hangover again!

Index

Hangover cures appear in **bold**.

Picture Credits — all photographs courtesy of The Kobal Collection
Film title, page number; stars; year of release, studio

American Dream, An 142; Eleanor Parker; 1966, Warner Brothers. Apartment, The, 176; Jack Lemmon; 1960, United Artists. Breakfast at Tiffany's, 64; Audrey Hepburn; 1961, Paramount. Circe the Enchantress, cover & 215; Mae Murray; 1924, Disney. Father of the Bride, 33; Spencer Tracy; 1950, MGM. Faithless, 74; Talulah Bankhead & Hugh Herbert, 1932, MGM. 1932, First National/ Warner Bros. Long Voyage Home, The, 104; Barry Fitzgerald, John Wayne & John Qualen; 1940, United Artists. Love on Toast, 188; Isabel Jewell & Stella Adler; 1937, Paramount. Mary, Mary, 34; Barry Nelson; 1963, Warner Bros. Merry Widow, The, 130; John Gilbert; 1925, Metro. Meet the Chump, 114; Hugh Herbert; 1941, Universal. Men, 140; Pola Negri; 1924, Famous Players/Lasky. New Babylon, The, 198; 1929; Sovkino. North by Northwest, 162; Cary Grant; 1959, MGM. Nothing Sacred, 132; Carole Lombard; 1937, Selznick/United Artists. Pillow Talk, 216; Rock Hudson & Tony Randall; 1959, Universal. Red-headed Woman, 144; Jean Harlow & Una Merkel; 1932, MGM. Scarlet Street, 100; Joan Bennett; 1945, Universal. Shadows of Paris, 90; Pola Negri; 1924, Paramount. Some Like it Hot, 186; Jack Lemmon & Marilyn Monroe; 1959, United Artists. Speak Easily, 166; Thelma Todd & Buster Keaton; 1932, MGM. Stage Door, 174; Ginger Rogers, Katherine Hepburn & Adolphe Menjou; 1937, RKO. That Way with Women, 92; Sydney Greenstreet & Martha Vickers; 1947, Warner Bros. That's My Boy, 61 & 152; Jerry Lewis & Eddie Mayehoff; 1951, Paramount. Three Stooges, The, 52; Larry Fine, Moe Howard, Curly Howard; The Kobal Collection. Tiger Shark, 164; Leila Bennett & Edward G. Robinson; Tonight or Never, 154; Gloria Swanson; 1931, Goldwyn/ United Artists. Tony Rome, 51; Sue Lyon; 1967, 20th Century Fox. Top Hat, 113; Edward Everett Horton; 1935, RKO. Underworld, 62; Evelyn Brent; 1927, Paramount. What Price Glory, 102; Dolores del Rio; 1926, 20th Century Fox. Wedding March, The, 184; Paramount. Wild Party, The, 72; Marceline Day, Joyce Compton, Clara Bow, & Shirley O'Hara; 1929, Paramount. You're Only Young Twice, 196; Jacqueline Mckenzie & Charles Hawtrey; 1950, MGM